IDEAS ABOUT SUBSTANCE

IDEAS ABOUT SUBSTANCE

ALBERT L. HAMMOND

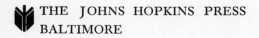 THE JOHNS HOPKINS PRESS
BALTIMORE

To Virginia, without whom not

Ill at press time, the author is especially grateful for the editorial help of his wife, Victor Lowe, Victoria Lincoln Lowe, John Young, and the Press.

CONTENTS

PUBLISHER'S NOTE

The history of ideas as a form of scholarly inquiry took shape at The Johns Hopkins University in the first half of the century. The man chiefly responsible was Arthur O. Lovejoy, whose twenty-eight years as professor of philosophy were spent promoting the historiography of the intellect. With two colleagues, George Boas and Gilbert Chinard, he founded the History of Ideas Club, where, in an atmosphere at once congenial and critical, visiting scholars might offer their interpretations of the development of the great ideas that have influenced civilization. Lovejoy was instrumental in founding the *Journal of the History of Ideas* in pursuit of the same end. And in his own writings he persistently and patiently charted the transformations which a seminal idea might undergo—over time, across disciplines, or within the intellectual development of an individual thinker.

When, with Carnegie Corporation support, The Johns Hopkins University inaugurated an imaginatively new program of adult education in 1962, it was a happy inspiration to build it around a set of graduate seminars in the history of ideas; for the History of Ideas Club itself had long before been described as "a sort of seminar where mature men and women learned new and valuable lessons." To be sure, this evening program has followed Lovejoy's spirit of inquiry rather than his own actual practice. Not all the seminars are concerned to pursue in detail the transformations of a single unit-idea. Rather, there is a shared view that no theory—at any time, in any field—is simply self-generated, but that it springs by extension or opposition from earlier theories advanced in the field, or is borrowed from theories in cognate fields, or is derived from the blending of hitherto separate fields into one. To pursue the unfolding of any theory in these terms (so the teachers in the seminars believe) allows a sophisticated and rigorous discussion of contemporary scholarship with an audience lacking previous specified knowledge. These notions are an extension, not an abuse, of Lovejoy's concern; he had never wasted effort on being unduly prescriptive except to call, hopefully, for cooperative scholarship in a venture so clearly beyond the reasonable capabilities of a single scholar.

This series of books, *Seminars in the History of Ideas*, is intended to provide a wider audience with a chance to participate in "a sort of seminar" similar to those in the University's program. Just as the teaching seminars themselves draw on the spirit rather than merely the letter of Lovejoy's original enterprise, so this published series extends beyond those topics already offered in the University's program. But all, nonetheless, reflect that intent with which Lovejoy so long persisted in his own work: "the endeavor to investigate the history, and thereby, it may be hoped, to understand better the nature, of the workings of the human mind."

PREFACE

The Animals They Come One By One

During the long years the Yankees were winning the pennants I used to ask Yankee lovers, or occasionally a Yankee hater, what it was he supposed he was admiring or deploring. The owners changed, the front office changed, the ground crew changed, managers, coaches, and of course players came and went. What was it that always won? One answer, not as bad as some, was that the pinstripes stayed. Yes, and the pinstripes did something. But a day came when the pinstripes lay inert on the shoulders, and the Yankees were just another ball club.

A more dangerous attack on man's reality was from the other side: not from the collection to which he belongs but from the ultimate very-little materials that are parts of him. This attack was classically mounted by Democritus: All is atoms in the void, plus their supervenient arrangements, arrangements of which neither the atoms nor the void has any care, pride, or record. We escaped this through the sophistication of Athens, especially the sagacity of Aristotle.

Aristotle, known for his doctrine that the soul is the "form" of the living thing, could take time to be derisive of Socrates' reincarnating soul; but he makes it clear that the soul must be the form of a living thing and that any mere arrangement of atoms (which he calls the doctrine of Democritus) cannot be soul, life, knowledge, goodness, or indeed anything except a spatial arrangement of atoms. And Aristotle makes this emphatic in what I take to be a most authoritative statement of his basic position (*Parts of Animals*, Book I).

But that was 2,300 years ago, and since the dominance of modern mathematical physics the attack has been renewed, constant; and the defense has been unsure. The defense, as often in modern philosophy, also suffers a bit of odd confusion when the old-time chief defender turns up somewhat ambiguously as an enemy agent or perhaps double-agent. For several generations there has been an easy fashion, coming chiefly I think from Bertrand Russell and "general semantics," of referring to Aristotelian logic and the subject-predicate proposition as a semeiotic excuse for our believing so obviously an unanalyzed familiarity as that the names of our children stand for continuingly real and separate persons. And, indeed, the subject-predicate Aristotelianism is also sometimes supposed to make us sure that when we have come into possession of a substantial subject we have something that cannot possibly change at all.

I know Lord Russell has read Aristotle. But Lord Russell has a charming ability to read in a text, especially a great one, less and other than most of us. Some of the others, I often feel, are just using slogans.

Aristotle there was. And he was a logician. So there is an Aristotelian logic. But I do not profess to know who now knows a very great deal about it. But Aristotle tells us a subtance can be in the subject, cannot be predicated; and in the simplest sense is something like this man, or this horse. Its chief mark that it is a substance is that it can and does change.

I think Aristotle is in danger of not being properly wary of the doctrine of the unchangingness of the predicate. This is Pythagoras, "the number theory of the idea," from which Aristotle dissociated himself in the Academy and of which he grew less wary once he was out of the controversy. Predicates as opposed to substances can be unchanging, and the glory of mathematical science probably rests on this. The number 2 is eternal and, with change for example, we can stipulate precision or set up a field-within-which so that what changes for Pythagoras is also changing for Robert Boyle or for Albert Einstein. Precision and abstraction are high mental abilities that we can, in the predicate, apply to the existent substances of the subject. (The common noun may do a similar trick in the subject.) But "I am tired" is a good subject-predicate proposition: and what is more changeable than the I or than the tiredness with which I am tired? That is a pleasant sentence because when it is used the subject is necessarily a substance, the statement is true, and a somewhat different statement is also being truthfully made: "I am at work."

If I conclude, as I do, that the world is composed of substantial individuals, existing with the characters they actually have, with parts they actually have, and in the media of the relationships of time, space, and causal connections which they actually have, is it of great import where we allot the word "substance," as nearer part or whole? I am convinced it is. But I shall not argue it or try to prove it here. We have the authority of T. S. Eliot that men feel hollow. The real answers here are apt to come from some of the many sciences now feeling a new need of the integralness of existence along with the new distinctions of function. It may be they will come from my friend Bentley Glass;[1] or from Michael Beer, or from another. Discriminatory intellect must discriminate à *outrance*. But intellect should be intelligent enough to have learned that knowing is far more than both intellect and intelligence, that knowing—like existing, choosing, loving—is to be done all in a piece.

> She was a phantom of delight
> When first she burst upon my sight.

1. He now has a book on science and ethics which I have not been able to read.

A lovely apparition sent
To be a moment's ornament.

. . .

I saw her upon nearer view
A spirit, yet a woman too;
Her household motions light and free,
Her step of virgin liberty.

. . .

And now I see with eye serene
The very pulse of the machine.
A traveler between life and death,
A being breathing thoughtful breath
And yet a spirit still and bright
With something of angelic light.

This poem would be nonsense if all stanzas were not known to be addressed to the same woman, known to be the same by her, by the author, and by many others. I can find nothing in Aristotle's *Organon*, or indeed anywhere else, that would have embarrassed the philosopher in writing this poem to Herpyllis. Except of course that he was not Wordsworth.

CHAPTER I

PRE-SOCRATIC PRE-EMPTIONS

When a child builds a house of blocks he knows the house is built of blocks, that even if it does not fall down he can knock it down and perhaps build it up again. It is often said that we can make an omelet of eggs but we cannot get the eggs out of the omelet. We know that one surface of one of those blocks we built with is a part of that block, but we cannot take the geometrical surface from the block: we can abstract it but not extricate it. We talk of a man's passions and his reason. We cannot extricate them or even get at them in the way we can the surface of a block. There are many kinds of parts and wholes. Some can be put together, taken apart, put together again. Some can be analyzed, clearly distinguished, but not separated. Some can be analyzed only with the addition of suspectable scaffolding to help the distinctions, or only with the loss of something that is in the whole but not in the analytic outcomes.

When we change a red slide for a green slide in the projector, there is change of quality, of color, on the screen. The colors of the sunset change by merging. A man walking across the room in a movie changes positions in rapid enough succession so as to give the cinematographic illusion of moving. All change of place can, by intellectual ingenuity, be so reduced, and, if Bergson objects and we ought not to forget Zeno, the calculus can be counted on to take care of the mathematics of it. The biologist sets growth as a character of life. Growth can be considered as a succession of larger sizes, although it may be questioned if this is adequate to what growth means to the child, or the parent. Living itself seems to involve change. So does knowing—I do not say "having knowledge." A large number, most, of the words with which we refer to the world and especially to action and undergoing, our own or another's, carry in their meaning a change that is more and other than a succession (accepting that as possible without "real" change) of states. Living, knowing, hungering, fearing, loving, wearying, wondering—what are their cross-sections, whereof they may be built, or even whereby they may be understood? This too may be called illusion.

How do we know such goings-on? I do not clearly know what "having knowledge" means, either as to the "having" or the "knowledge," but I think I know, and that I know that I know in knowing—say a headache. "Nur wer die Sehnsucht kennt"—he knows longing in longing and, in that, he comes to know something beyond. But he has no visual, auditory, tactile, olfactory, or gustatory "data" of longing; and any internal state is a state of change if not just poetic or mythical. What Berkeley said of cause, and Hume repeated with embroidery, is true of many notions: they are not observed. How do we know when we are hungry? Schopenhauer says one learns more of gravity by standing among the buttresses or under the nave of a cathedral and sympathizing with the aspiration and labor of the stones than by reading Newton. I think it would be inhuman to give up either one. The ordinary fellow, rather than yearning in cathedrals, may find it sufficient to carry his suitcase upstairs and find it easier to sympathize with himself.

When I was a graduate student in philosophy I went to a learned meeting and afterward reported, "Everything was intelligible to everyone and nothing was understood by anyone." That pleased me, stayed, and led on. The verdict used a distinction between intelligible and understandable; the distinction made it intelligible that understanding might be—and seemed to make me understand that understanding should be—something more than putting under the syntactic validity of intelligibility a set of clear and distinct perceptions, something more than supplying data for the argument and an argument for the data. But there was not, and still is not, an understanding of just what that more is.

I had already given up the perceptual dualism of my teacher Arthur Lovejoy. He had elaborately and acutely made it as intelligible to me as any theory of perception; but I became aware that I just could not honestly say I believed, when I looked at him, or heard the wind, or felt the handlebar of my bicycle or the push of its pedals uphill, that I was seeing or hearing or feeling or having an idea. So I knew I was a realist, and I have become more so. I rejoiced that there was a push of realism in American philosophy—Morris Cohen and W. P. Montague came to Hopkins as visiting professors, and they were realists—but it receded, and my support of a trend became a complaint that since Hume a great need of philosophy has been more realism.

Meanwhile I was developing my feeling that our knowing needs a larger basis of acquaintance than is allowed by the orthodox philosophy and psychology coming down from the eighteenth century. Especially in years of teaching "logic and scientific method," my very admiration of the cleanness of objective observation and measurement made me wonder if success within this area does not foreshorten acceptance of what may be beyond, and limit scrutiny of the sources of some of scientific method itself. Surely induction has some more penetrating assurance than that of the enumeration or criticism of repeated separate items of presentation. How do we know cause, how do we know a memory is memory, how do we know each other, how do we know we are hungry, how do we know we are alive, how do we know the knowledge of good and evil?

Then at times there was a bit of worry that my two allegiances were contrary. My realism accented the objective; these how-do-we-know queries seemed to invite the subjective. My realism had become aware of itself in the midst of the eighteenth-century problem of perception—the perception of objects (which I believed to be things) with qualities and relations in space and time. But these other acquaintances, of cause, of hunger, of good and evil, are some mind's acquaintances, and are a mind's acquaintances with something that is not a thing and is not that mind itself, even if what the mind is acquainted with is its own contrivance.

The two recognitions of insufficiency have, it is true, worked against each other at times in the history of philosophy. When American realism receded, it may have been in part because of Whiteheadian and other calls for a wider and richer acquaintance.

But I have come to think the two are ultimate allies; that they find a common ground in the doctrine of substance—what is really there—as an integral existence which endures and changes and as such responds, acts and suffers, chooses.

If we are called on to interpret the question, "what is really there?" we can hope the word "really" escapes some of the well-known badness of "real"—much of the pretentiousness if not the equivocality—and the word "there" seems to limit us, helpfully, to the world of existence, fencing off the hopes and fears, the values beyond those hopes and fears, which are a real, perhaps the "most real," factor in our acquaintance and living, and also fencing off the assertion of a Platonist or mathematician that the forms, ideas, numbers, characters, "eternal objects," are the most real of reals. Fears do much, but without the fearer are nothing. The number may be eternal, but in that case cannot move or be moved. What is really there can, at least in varying degree, do without what is here; but can also do to and be done to by what is here. This is not to assume anything as to the nature of "physical space" and not to forget that it may be denied that there is anything really there.

The word "substance," I believe, was first meant to do the same job as the phrase "what is really there"; and through most of its mostly ancient and honorable usage continued to be so meant—with dangerous waverings. But it is a learned word and lately of ill repute. We must presently give it some stipulations and look at the history of both the word and the problem.

The problem of what is really there is raised by the official first philosophers, the Milesians, and stays on. There is no need to call it the only problem of philosophy or the basic one, except "ontologically," as part of metaphysics, "beyond physics." Value, as said, must be first in the sense of importance; and knowledge, as the "critical philosophy" argued, must be first in the sense of clarification. It may be that each has to depend upon the others. We philosophers, and nonphilosophers if any, have, do, are all three: we exist, and existing we know and choose. Putting it this way is to suggest that I feel Aristotle was right in making the category of substance fundamental.

We want to know about the history of the word "substance" and about the answers that have been given and the answer we should give to the question traditionally associated with "substance": what is really there?

There is now a fairly distinct threefold division of verbal usage and of opinion among the scientists, the philosophers, and the general users of language.

1. With scientists and the popular writing that follows science and the ordinary talk on scientific subjects, the source and the most frequent use of "substance" is from chemistry: "chemical substances" are sub-superficial stuffs or materials

such as chlorophyl, haemin, proteins, magma. We can be comfortable in this usage in part because these substances are not meant as *the* substance since they are all clearly compositions or concretes. They are taken as substances in respect of the individual thing, plant, or animal in which they are; still more normally as substances in respect of the more familiar and more familiarly handled material in which they are. In this strain we are not apt to call wood or alpha particles substances.

As to a fundamental stuff in the tradition of physical philosophy or physics, either the scientists did not want to be bothered in the recent yesterday or they expressly did not want any such final stuff of things. Then the Einsteinians, still without much use of the word "substance," were apt to be Pythagorean and formalize what is really there into space-time, geometry, and number, and so dilute the existentiality of their substance, the substantial becoming adjectival. The Copenhagen interpretation of quantum physics pushed its basic stuff to the position I used to find (and Werner Heisenberg finds) in the Milesians of sixth century B.C. Greece. In each case, however, and still more in both, there is apparent a revival of a real substantialism of the stuff variety, a quite new theory of basic material of a freer and richer potentiality than earlier materialisms. This is achieved by the optionalism of non-Euclidean geometries in relativity theory, and by the wave-particle-probability optionalism of quantum theory. Meanwhile the word "substance" goes on generally in this sort of discourse—even in Heisenberg's usage—meaning "chemical substances."

2. Among the philosophers perhaps the most significant from this point of view is Whitehead, who rejects "substance" because he accepts a definition of it as unchanging and he wants process. Being an experience man, although declaring himself a realist, he seems to more realistic realists

to dilute what is there (like and unlike the Einsteinians) when he makes "occasions" of experienced content or occasions of experiencing (either seems able to be or to get along without the other), the subjectivity and the brevity of the occasions being hard to make into any enduringness through change, and harder to make into interaction among themselves, except for those in one train or "society" which may be thought of as carrying predecessors on or being represented in successors.

The positivists and more orthodox followers of the tradition of Hume reduce both matter and person or thing either to phenomenalism (certain orderings among impressions) or to formalism and logicism.

The existentialists have the word "existence" and emphasize freedom and choice and doing-and-suffering—good marks of a sort of substantialism—but are even more subjective (except maybe Heidegger) than Whitehead and so lose enduringness, independence, and much of the thereness of old-fashioned substance.

The personalists sometimes remind us of the original assertion of Aristotle that substance in the truest sense is a thing like this man or this horse. So now and then do some of the English ordinary language philosophers. But in England Hume still scares, and the American personalists lack a full base of rebellion—which the existentialists have—or a base inside the establishment. And these too are wary of the word.

3. In literature and common sense the old meanings of the word, multiple but centered, and approbative, remain. So the Whiteheadian who has been lecturing on the needlessness of substance will go home and praise the substance of the editorial in the evening paper.

In the long and curious history of language some words stay around, and some even stay with the same meaning.

But many words go, and almost all words change meanings. Some words are more important for one person or another, say a philosopher. And a shift in meaning may not only be an annoyance to an old-fashioned fellow or a historian but also may significantly influence theory, belief, and action. It will usually have this doctrinal effect, illicit because hidden, by keeping some relic of its earlier meaning while definitely changing its reference—so that the thing to which it newly refers is given some share of its original meaning. Thus "atom," originally meaning the indivisible particle, if any, came in early modern science to refer to the particle chemically constitutive of the elements. When in time we split the "atom," there seemed to be a sort of logical as well as technological breakthrough or affront.

It is still a vanity to fight about words, or the fate of words. But sometimes, as in the case of "much study," it is a needful "vanity and vexation of spirit" to fight against bad usage or to put on record a warning of the old and the new meaning and reference.

"Substance" may not be the most important instance of such a word; but it may be. Philosophers may be said always, perhaps necessarily, to want to know what is really there. Such is the original meaning of "substance," and it is still visibly in the background of the twenty-three uses listed in the New English Dictionary. But even in Aristotle its reference—that in what-was-there for Aristotle which he thought most truly deserved the good word "substance"—wavered; and out of this wavering, perhaps, came divagations and embroideries, and, in philosophic and scientific theory, some fixations even partly contradictory. In the same age as "atom," with a sudden and wider jump, substance became identified with the stuff, especially the chemical stuff, of which a thing is made. Or with the philosophers, much affected by chemical substances as well as by Descartes' "material substance," the word has come to mean what does not change, although Aristotle's basic characterization of it is as what can and does change. This alters the meaning, and after a while the alteration in meaning becomes a denial that there is any reference of the word to anything in existence since there is nothing there that does not change. Yet the deniers of substance still want to be able to distinguish what is really there from what somehow is unreal or less real and from what somehow is not there.

"Substance" has been since the Greek οὐσία, and still is generally, a "good" word: "a man of substance," "the sum and substance," "substantially so," "a substantial meal," "of more substance," "give of your substance," "wasted his substance in riotous living." Students are apt to be a bit incredulous when I say that in recent technical philosophy, some philosophers, perhaps most, find it a "bad" word, and that others not directly involved, whom they influence, are fashionably apt to deride substance or are chary of paying any deference.

And yet in all its many general-use meanings it has kept the core of reality, of the relatively more real, and the natural as the existent: hence the independent, the enduring, the more than subjective, the nonartificial, the effective, the affected, the important, what is there. These are "good" notions; the philosopher can hardly upstage them.

In time most words generalize, lose their edges, widen out and flatten down. So "category"—which for 2,200 years kept its learnedness and its Aristotelian high-and-mightiness even while shifting variously its technical application—was suddenly in this century made the prey of psychologist, salesman, advertiser, quiz show, and newsman, and now the poor thing is just an overworked word for any sort of sort. I have read of a "category of tugboats in the Baltimore harbor." "Firm" meant an association of individuals who remain in-

dividuals but work together and have a sort of group existence, as a firm of lawyers or architects. Now it is the news-
paper word for any business, company or corporation. I
have read of someone buying ("purchasing") a firm, despite
the outlawing of slavery.

Other words come to apply, within their meaning, to
more specific or individual things or notions which may turn
out later not to deserve that meaning or to which later
theorists may not want to grant that meaning. So with
"atom," and "ether," and the "Donation of Constantine,"
and that "great fish," the whale.

"Substance" (what is real and existent) came in Descartes
and his successors to specify and, I think, falsify its meaning
so that its trait of enduringness withdrew into unchangingness (Descartes was a mathematician and mathematical physicist), and its comparative or relative independence pushed
on to absolute independence. So then in chemistry the word
is applied to the stuff or stuffs of which things are made.
Twentieth-century science uses the word easily in the plural
(chemical "substances") but mostly has no absolute stuff
and needs none. Nor do most philosophers think there is
any unchanging material substrate; and, denying this, they
are apt to say they are denying substance. For my part, I do
not believe there is any unchanging material substrate. And
if there were, I should not call it substance. Yet substance I
am sure there is, and indeed must be.

Meanwhile, after the meaning of "substance" and the
theory of matter had narrowed to meet in something probably
altogether insubstantial, the major ingenuity of modern
philosophy developed. By this it is decided that the existence
of mind and the existence of matter, now purified and
separated, are, indeed can only be, found in and constructed
out of the presented ideas, perceptions, impressions, phenomena (perhaps Thomas Hobbes's first word, "phantasms,"

is the best), experience (in the more recent fashion). So matter and mind, body and soul, I and it, are themselves ideas; not ideas for any mind, since it would seem a mind for which an idea is an idea is itself something more than an idea; and not an idea of any thing, except other ideas or ideal constructs of ideas.

Even here there will be some theory of what is more and what is less really there. The phenomenalist normally wants a distinction between dream and waking. In the sort of world Socrates and Theaetetus attribute to Protagoras, some opinion is better than another even if not more true. Even that "strange guest" of Nietzsche's, nihilism, rejects some commands as peculiarly mythical. Nevertheless, in such a world as has been fashionable since Hume (although it may not have been "really" his world), and with the acceptance of "substance" as meaning the unchanging, what is asserted to be really there is not going to be that sort of substance and, surely, in older and better meanings of "substance" it is going to be pretty insubstantial.

A trouble is that change, too, is going to be hard to account for. Santayana would say we are here given a tapestry of changeless "essences." Change might be said to be a "cinematographic illusion," the flicker of the many stills of the movie. But it is hard to account for illusion when there is no mind with an enduring acquaintance with change to be illuded. So Bergson, and Whitehead, and others with a feeling for substance, struggle.

It is hardly fair to blame the not unnatural translation of substance as stuff on Descartes—who has earned his title as father of modern philosophy by being always handy to blame for whatever it is we dislike in modern philosophy—since it is clearly played with (if usually rejected) by Aristotle, the definer and answerer of the problem of substance, and is present, as it were inversely, in the first philosophers and physicists, the Milesians. Inversely because here the meanings cannot be said to be confused: they are just beginning to be separated out. We are not told what the Milesians were up to; not told by them. Our modern books tell us their aim was scientific—to give a natural explanation of the natural world (whatever "natural" means)—and philosophic —to discern the real, as that of which explanation is intended. Each of these two aims, scientific and philosophic, may use, bow to, reject, or be critical of the other. The two begin to show themselves, and the former—the motive of explanation—tends, as intellectually the more clearly needed, to take dominance in the second of the Milesians, Anaximander. But my feeling and belief is that the first, Thales, was not so much setting off on the "problem of the constitution of matter" because he thought it basic in scientific explanation as he was announcing a vision of the real nature of nature.

When Thales said "All things are water" he meant that all things are "made of" water in the sense that we are made of eyes, and muscles, and blood; and also that the table is made of wood; but not in the sense that either is made of atoms or electrical energy. Water is not recondite but immediate. Water more than any other part of the actual has the important character of things, not only has body but has power and a sort of primitive life. "All things are full of gods." Doubtless Thales was impressed by the fact that water can be seen turning into ice and steam; and he would take water from among these three because, certainly on the Ionian coast, water is the normal form. But Aristotle tells us, I am sure truthfully, that Thales was moved by the fact that water moves, that moist warmth is characteristic of life, that all seeds are moist.

Thales was great not only by the firstness of his genius but by its priorness: he came before analysis had prepared the artificial parting of the ways in which he could go wrong.

I used to say that one has to start the study of substance with Thales although he was looking not for substance but for the stuff of all things. Of these three propositions—it is good to begin with Thales; he was not looking for substance; he was looking for stuff—the first is true but the second is partly true only in the way that the third is partly false. The meanings of substance and stuff had not been analytically arrived at, to be separated or equated. Thales, like any philosopher, was looking for what is real. The Milesian bent of mind inclined toward what became the stuff identification of substance. But this was not express; and I think it would have been refused, by Thales and perhaps by Anaximander and Anaximenes, if it had been made express that stuff was to be divested—as in the later materialistic tradition, or just as firmly in the later tradition of the meaning of matter for the anti-materialists—of as much as possible of the non-stuff predicates, notably character and quality, power and life.

When I was a boy in West Baltimore, the Park Board built a fountain in Harlem Park. It was a deep, heavily walled, circular pool, some twenty-five feet across, with heavy marble balustrade, and heavily overarched with big trees. It had a single wide nozzle in the center, and just before the spray fixture was brought uptown for attachment (so the story was) the water was turned on. As the pool filled, the water reached the level of the nozzle, covered it six inches, and established a rhythm: the stream, forcing its way through, urged the water up the sides of the pool and then the mass of the water coming down again piled up in the center and cut off the heavy stream. It was an Old Faithful of steady period, thirty or forty seconds. It was named the Geyser in the neighborhood and soon so known across the city.

The nozzle was big, the stream heavy; and, as it was cut off below, the water already in air hung suspended a moment and fell back with a heavy plop rather than a splash. The spray was not at the fountain but around the pool, the leeward side of which was always wet. The children, the adult passers-by, even the officials were amused and bemused. And the intended attachment was sent back downtown.

When now I read or talk about Thales, I think of the Geyser. It brought me up on, it made me feel, the potent reality of water—as Walt Whitman on Paumanok shore felt the wave "out of the cradle endlessly rocking."

I did not always think of the Geyser with Thales. It took me time to get the feel of Milesianism, its reaching for substance as well as for stuff. The books say that Thales, the great naturalist and generalizer, wanted a simple material of which all things are made. I do not doubt it. But if we turn back from our late-won lust and confidence in building up to living things from an abstractly pure geometrical or algebraic matter, perhaps we can with Thales, looking at water—and the magnet—say the reality of the world is in living things, "generated not made," and, "All things are full of gods"—the heaviness of body, the life of its lift, its force, its direction, its aspiration, its fall and weariness.

I think Thales is splendid: first philosopher of what is, first not only in time but in rank of rightness. He announces the thereness of a common nature but keeps it actual by keeping it alive. But his splendid rightness is the rightness of the road before the fork is reached. He grasps the fact and the problem before the problem is opened up. Anaximander is the genius who takes the decisive step and by its very "justice," the justice he appeals to, misleads most of those who came later. For he could hardly see, without quadruple genius, and they generally failed to see, that his just and justified step took him away from substance into the analysis of substance along that dimension that we mean by stuff. Anaximander saw that if we mean by Thales' question to ask what is the ultimate stuff, material, component of things, in the simple sense in which a table is made of wood, then we cannot nominate any actual familiar stuff in the world, for if we do, another stuff can say, "Why not me? You are unjust. You say water turns into steam; does not steam turn into water?" That of which all things are made must be no present thing, must go beyond, beneath all visible candidates, and ultimately beyond all namable or thinkable characters' existence or potentiality, must be the "boundless," the uncharacterized from which all characters are "shaken out," although no character or characters are previously there. But Anaximander knew there are characters, is character, in this world although there is none in his boundless. He is regularly praised for the firstness and the elaboration of his "naturalistic cosmology." Good Milesian as he is, he thinks of the stuff as real and lets the first shaking out of character, form, individuality, differentiation go unexpounded. So later the probable descendant of his boundless, Aristotle's prime matter, "yearns for form as the female for the male," although as such it has not even the first qualities of hot, cold, wet, dry. Without warmth or frigidity it yearns. I think it is Anaximander who gives the "Copenhagen interpretation"; he is the Niels Bohr of the first physics.

Pythagoras does it from the other direction. "All things are number." All things are not merely the bounded, all things are the bounds. If we ask a physicist what is the constitution of matter and he says energy or electricity, we get a Milesian (but a "sophisticatedly" Milesian) answer; and if he is a follower of Bohr and Heisenberg, we get it in Anaximanderian terms. If he talks of atomic numbers and differential equations, we get a Pythagorean answer. Yet, although there is no doubt of Pythagoras' honesty, he cannot have completely meant his "All things are numbers." In addition to the numbers, there seems to be "an outside darkness" and the soul. The Pythagoreans speak of an outside darkness that is drawn into the bright and shining numbers to make this world, the cosmos. Pythagoras' personal and moral and religious teaching, the soul—the reality and overriding importance of the soul, which goes from one bodily life to another, which is the bearer of knowledge and ignorance; of virtue and vice, merit and blame; which grows better or worse, and which by these very facts is assuredly characterized and richly formed, a character in the human sense—is not a character in the logical sense, is not a predicate, an adjective, a shape, a form; is not a number. Numbers, poor splendid things, are eternal; the soul is immortal. Some later Pythagoreans tried to define the soul in numerical terms, and Socrates, a true Pythagorean, sufficiently disposes of the "soul as a harmony": if the soul is a real soul, that is, a Pythagorean or Socratic soul.

(I am not prepared to say this is the same as Aristotle's argument that the Aristotelian theory of the soul as the form of a living body makes nonsense of transmigration. Aristotle's form here, or "first entelechy of a body naturally having life," is expressly something more than a shape, an arrangement, a number—the theory he attributes to Democritus and rejects in the *Parts of Animals* [*I*, 1, 640b30 ff.].)

To be sure, Pythagoras is an extraordinarily many-sided philosopher. Born on the island of Samos, just offshore from Miletus, he carried the Ionian scientific habit of mind across the Greek world, going as a boy or youth with his father, Mnesarchus, to the southern coast of Italy, the instep of the boot, the cities of Sybaris, Metapontum, Croton, where the Orphic cults, probably the older Mediterranean religion, were known and growing. Thus he did not bring with him the secularism of Ionia and its scant belief or interest in the soul; but he combined his scientific vision with a vision of the worldly and otherworldly life of the soul and declared the ultimate salvation of the latter in the perfection of the former. We free ourselves from barbarism and worldliness into competence in this world and others by understanding of what is, and the best understanding is mathematics. Bertrand Russell in the far-off days of "The Free Man's Worship" was being Pythagorean, if not just so. The father of mathematics, Pythagoras is also the father of musicology; and he is the founder of perhaps the longest-lived of all secret societies; the propounder of rules dietetic, superstitious, and purely Pythagorean (those for which no other reason can be thought of, one of which I try always to keep); the theorist of the three lives (those who take care of the crowds at the Olympic Games, the competitors, the lookers-on) and so the father of Greek snootiness and of classicism in art and enjoyment; the background of Socratic ethics; the founder of the Italian school of medicine with the theory of the temperaments, tension, and tonics; the metaphysician of means and extremes, 6-8-9-12, the regular polyhedra, elementary (atomic) weights and numbers, the music of the spheres; the great teacher of otherworldliness in the world's business, of intoxication (beer, wine, poetry, music, mathematics) in religion, and so of the Methodist revival, of the danger of routine and respectability. Among the paradoxes: as the background of Greek snootiness we may find him behind the striking Greek failure to do much with arithmetic; and as the background of Methodism we may find him behind the United States prohibition amendment.

Still, as ontologist he seems the complement of Anaximander. They see a radical analytic distinction of two ingredients—rather two egredients—content and form, mass and shape, the boundless and number—and each proclaims the one he likes. Their teacher, Thales, had both. And so, I think, does substance.

I am a substance. I live. How do I know I live? I think

I am a body, have Anaximanderian stuff, Aristotelian substrate. Last summer late in the surf at Ocean City, I was attacked by a surfboard just after its rider washed out. I had seen the board and I believed its materiality; but my body itself felt, hurt for a week. I can argue that such awareness of changing external shapes and of intracutaneous pain can be taken as sufficient evidence of being alive. But surely that basic assurance or experience (here a word I dislike and distrust seems to fit) of living, now briefly focused, is more than an argument, more even than that Cartesian "I think therefore I am," which he protests is too immediate to be regarded as an argument. Hume's trick of tabulating the "impressions" of sight, hearing, touch, taste, and smell, plus pain or pain-pleasure, and then arguing, with no possibility allowed of any other acquaintance, surely wore insufferably thin a hundred years ago, although it still afflicts us—and, it is only fair to add, sometimes protects us.

Heraclitus of Ephesus, Miletus' neighboring city to the north, was the first rebel against science. He used to be hailed as notably scientific because he believed in change. And yet he came after Thales and his energetic and transmogrifying water, and those who hailed him lived in the nineteenth-century days of reversible Newtonian-Laplacean physics, when Darwin was restraining even biological change in regularity. Heraclitus' indignation for his scientific predecessors was similarly, but less inaccurately, unfair to the life in Thales' teaching and the soul in Pythagoras'. The laudable objectivity of the scientific motive in those great originators led them to objectify even the metaphysical vision behind the scientific and to allow the natural focusing of their own and their followers' contemplative interest and curiosity on the more objective scientific theory. So Milesianism became a theory of the constitution of matter and Pythagoreanism, a theory of extremes—means and the regular polyhedra as explanatory of heard music, observed physics, and calculated astronomy. Just "a knowledge of many things," Heraclitus says.

Heraclitus is indignant because he thinks his scientist predecessors and contemporaries have tried to take from him the sensuous-sensual qualities in which he glories and still more because they took away the enduring self in which he feels real and part of the great self of all things. He is the philosopher of change because he knows his identity is not the identity of a number. He is the philosopher of the enduring because he knows he is not a difference or a bundle or succession of different numbers or descriptions or stuffs. "It is wise to harken . . . and know that all things are one."

Mr. W. K. C. Guthrie remarks that Heraclitus is the first to cast suspicion on the trustworthiness of the senses. The remark is just, but seems to me very incomplete. Heraclitus is skeptic, relativist; and in all things pulls no punches. Of the senses directly he says, "Eyes and ears are bad witnesses." They are bad witnesses but precious enjoyments. They are bad witnesses but still witnesses, and our only ones on the scene. They are bad because they are apt to focus attention on the separate qualities or on the inconstancy of quality and fail to see that even the inconstancy would lapse but for persistence, fail to get through to what is changing, fail to let us remind ourselves that they are avenues not only from the world but to ourselves. He is the philosopher of change surely enough because he emphasized that change is integral with the sameness of the enduring.

He is enough of a Greek and an intellectual at times to "think" that the best part of the self is the "thinking" part, the fire, which is also the fire of the world; and even at times to suggest a confusion of the "common," which is the true object of thinking, with the thinking common fire of the world. And yet the doctrine of the "common" as the logical and objective—as opposed to the subjective "world of his own" into which the sleeper "turns aside" and as opposed to the subjective-objective world of perceived things of which we all see different sides and angles—is itself, whatever its place in the Heraclitan personalism, one of his surest claims to originality and acuteness.

With the doctrine of the real and changing "one," that all things change and there is no change except of things, Heraclitus is the first to announce the doctrine of substance as substances, as changing individuals. But he does not use the word. That remains for Aristotle: "Substance in the truest sense is something like this man or this horse."

I do not think Heraclitus was the first to feel or believe this. With the assurance of most philosophers—feeling their views are "really" those of common sense—I believe we all start out that way. The child never doubts that he is one and enduring and changing. Then he goes to school and studies arithmetic and logic and chemistry and in college he is shocked to wonder whether he has "identity."

Aristotle also was the first to give an analysis of change, which the philosopher of change had not bothered about. Μεταβολή, he says, may be change of place, change of quality, or change of substance, as either growth and decay or (possibly) coming into being and passing away. It may be significant that change of place, which is most important or sole for (Cartesian) physics (not Bacon, or Bergson), seems least important for substantialism, as external to the moving thing. And in any case, Aristotle's analysis of change, still useful and used, has been apt, like all analyses, to externalize for the uses of observation and its scientific story. Heraclitus would probably want more. He would at least wonder whether change of personal character (and sameness as well, since we should have a parallel analysis of sameness) is taken care of under change of quality as that has come to be understood. There is that first-level change when the now-angry man becomes calm and that second-level change when the characteristically irascible man becomes serene. (It may be that the sometimes warm disagreement as to whether God changes could be eased. The Jew, who is most apt to accent "and still the same," talks of change, even locomotion, in the Old Testament. What we all may want is the last rubric of dependability above. John Bowring's hymn, "Chance and change are busy ever,/Man decays and ages move;/But His mercy waneth never," offers our undependability dependability. But what does not "wane" allows a sort of comparison to the moon. And mercy, if any good to us, is active. What change is there in the stationary traveler when "the mariner, in his fixedness and loneliness, yearneth toward the journeying moon, which still journeyeth and still sojourneth"?)

Parmenides breaks in from the West, from Elea the big Greek city farthest up the west coast of Italy—Parmenides, the most high and mighty dialectician of our philosophers, breaks in with the annoying voice of logic. "There is just one question. 'Is it, or is it not?' If all things are water, then anything that is not water is not. So be honest and do not talk of water turning into anything for, if it turns into, it turns into that which is not. Nor is there any nothing into which it can move and wherever it might move it is already there. 'Nor was it ever nor will it be but it is, altogether.' And it cannot have come into being nor can it pass away, for there is no nothing from which it could have come or into which it could go, and 'what cause could have made it arise later rather than sooner?' 'So is becoming extinguished and change of bright color.' And 'it is all one to me where I begin for I shall come back there again.' And this is not merely for water. Indeed water already implies internal characters and external contraries and all this is impossible.

What we have to consider is quite simply what is. What is is; there is no is not. 'What can be thought and that for the sake of which thought is are the same.' "

He is obviously wrong. But he seems to say that he does not care about what is obvious as long as he sees what is necessary. What he does not tell us (only the first and most radical of a long and perhaps endless line in history of failures to fill in) is how appearance, error, illusion is possible in the world that Parmenides announces as necessary.

He is not wrong, it seems to me, in the thesis that any stuff or material or basic-component theory of the world must have more than one component. And history since Parmenides, with occasional forays into the country he forbids, has backed him up. And this has worked out at times unfavorably to the word "substance." As with the Milesians, there is a natural tendency in the search for what is really there to poke into what things are made of. And then we talk at once of "a" basic stuff and "the" basic stuff. This may be only or mostly the proper love of simplicity in explanation; but there seems a special tendency to one in explanation by stuff. So we could rest easy a generation ago when we could feel that the electron was somehow the component of the proton; and so soon after Parmenides, when empty space moved openly on stage, it seemed, and still seems, not quite on a level with the matter moving through it. Is space material or not? And so some, probably without realizing it themselves, feel that if they say substance, they must say stuff; if they say stuff, they must say fundamental stuff; if they say that, they must say there is just one; and saying that, they see Parmenides wagging his finger.

By temperament Parmenides is an abstractionist. He is doing more than telling stuff-theorists to have more than one sort of stuff. His argument is that we must go on to, and must stop with, what is; and that which is, is, and is necessarily one as what is. I think this argument is invalid. But its invalidity is not easily and validly exposed. It is a commonplace to say that Plato dealt with it in the *Sophist*—with the doctrine of the existential and the predicative uses of the verb "to be" and of the "participation" of Ideas. He did— brilliantly, profoundly, difficultly, and incompletely. The topic also calls in the full theory of classification—classification which Aristotle practiced superbly but curiously did little to expound. We note here only that the generalizing process—from the individual "across the line" into the realm of classes, up from the lowest species through successive genera to the neighborhood of the category and then to the category, and beyond to the *summum genus* that is not a genus—all involves leaps and losses. Even being is not a competent *summum genus* since it does not take nonbeing into account; even the already-actual-isness of being cannot be used as a stuff from which the world can be thought of as made; it can only be abstracted from a world of individuals and particulars we find to start our knowing with. This is true of knowing; it is as true of creation; or so it seems to me. I know that great oaks from little acorns grow, and we may all have evolved from a primeval "soup" (with space and motion)—but not from being.

The atomism of Leucippus and Democritus, masterpiece of simplicity and elegance and in the mainstream of Western physics until now, takes the "One" of Parmenides and makes the least possible change and the most radical possible change. Accept the being of what-is-not in the fact of empty space and break up the fissureless "One" into very many, very little, pieces in motion. Within the atom keep Eleatic purity: no motion, no quality, no possible crevice. But externally the atom is in motion, without need of applied force, in motion haphazardly and with no up or down (forget the later moralist atomism of Epicurus and the Roman Lucretius with its "like a snowstorm"). The atom has size, shape, position, motion—the mathematical characters—and since, as Eleatic, it cannot merge or alter on impact, it follows its hard nature and some few, very simple, laws of geometrical mechanics (cf. the early modern concern over the impact of two perfectly rigid bodies). Develop whirlpool motion and we soon have nebulae, solar systems, ups and downs, more and more elaborate and complex agglomerations and constructions of atoms. All, substantially, is still atoms and the void.

Now this beautiful theory is the perfecting of the mathematical form of Pythagoras, dropping off the substantial soul; and of the stuff of Anaximander, dropping off the "hylozoism" of Miletus. There is propriety in the tradition that Leucippus was a Milesian who came to Abdera, on the northern shore of the Aegean, and taught Democritus. Thus analysis, and acuteness of imagination, has proceeded to a perfected platform for mathematical physics as a basis for all science. Its very elegance within, however, poses the philosophic problem of how to get outside to any other: how to emerge, how to move from a pure geometry and abstract matter and motion and space to the life, the knowing, the qualities, the goods and bads of what we set out to explain and of what we are.

Atomism inherits this difficulty from its "father Parmenides." Parmenides traveled to Athens with his follower Zeno and talked with the young Socrates, asked him about the newfangled "Idea," how it could be both one and many. We want to ask Parmenides how within his "One" he can account for the seeming differences of Italy, seas, and Attica; for the seeming motion of his journey—not to mention how we seem to be moved by those never-existent motions. With the birth of motion after the marriage of the geometrical what-is of the atom and the geometrical what-is-not of space, we get physics; but we still wonder: how does this beautifully bare ontology account for acquaintance, quality, response to quality and value? The history books call all these subjective, mental, a desirable naturalization of the "illusion," which the books invoke to help Parmenides. But where among the atoms in the void can the subjective grow; how does one shape have awareness of another; and why should a shape, no matter how complicated, be for or against its own shape or change of shape or another shape? Disruption is pain and we shun it, says atomism. This is surely so for a living thing; but the void is void, the atom is eternal, the shape of a billion atoms is utterly outer to the atoms, is at most truly predicative not substantial. "Emergism" has emerged. But it seems just an adding in of the mystery by a little at a time.

To be sure the atom, the Democritean boundless, is in its simplicity quite precisely bounded. It keeps the mathematical nonqualitative qualities of extension, at least pseudoexistence, space-time occupancy, and exclusiveness. And so Werner Heisenberg says: "This implies his concept of the atom cannot explain geometry, extension in space, or existence, because it cannot reduce these to something more fundamental. The modern Copenhagen quantum view of the elementary particle with regard to this point seems more consistent and radical." [1] Thus Francis Bacon often praises Democritus' use of "dissection" as against the "abstraction" of Plato and Aristotle;[2] Bacon first praises Democritus for making Cupid (the atom) naked but not formless and then finds fault with the form Democritus gives him. Really, the Baconian objection is to the eternality and geometrical simplicity of the atom's motion and of the atom's shape.

1. *Physics and Philosophy* (New York, 1958), p. 70.
2. *Principles and Origins of Nature, According to the Fables of Cupid and Heaven.*

CHAPTER II

ATHENIAN ELABORATION

Tradition talks of Socrates and Plato as patrons of some difficult idea known as the "Idea," as arguers on knowledge and morals and beauty, as "idealists." So the student puzzles over "participation" and tries to make up a two-level world of a perfect horse and unreal sense-world horses trying to "imitate" the perfect one, the "Idea." Well, they (Socrates, I think) discovered the "Idea," the "Form," the character as distinguished from the thing; and one can not blame them for being enthusiasts for what may well be the greatest of philosophic insights. The idea of the "Idea" is discernible in Pythagoras' "numbers" and, indeed, that acute woman Eve probably knew, even if Gabriel did not tell her, that the same adjective belongs to more than one thing and that one thing has more than one adjective. But for all their enthusiasm, I cannot find any evidence that they were ever bemused by notions of the exemplar horse who "of course is a thoroughbred"; and I cannot find any evidence that they denied the bodily world (Socrates, notably, was a very bodily man); and the soul was as much their insistence as was the "Idea" (Socrates was a very soulful man).

In the *Timaeus*—that late dialogue in which I see Plato writing a sort of first textbook in the history of Greek philosophy and in cosmology for his students—the Demiurge fashions the soul of the world before its body; the ideas are there for the pattern, but body, too, is there for the making of the world's body, and that soul-encircled body is, when made, really there and in motion. "Now that which comes to be must be bodily." "Now that which is actual is necessarily corporeal" (31b, trans. Cornford, Jowett).

Socrates is Pythagorean and with Pythagoras can say and love to say that all things are number. Yet the soul is not a number and it is that to which and for which the bright and shining numbers are knowledge and salvation as the soul goes from life to life and from body to body. So for Socrates the soul is that which lives, has lived, will live; essentially knows and in knowing turns toward beauty and what is good and so can love; it can grow in knowledge and virtue but is continually in danger through ignorance and false knowledge, shrewdness and vanity, and through its bodily career of worldly pressures is in danger of degeneration. Metaphysical and existential optimism of body, soul, science, and worship; worldly pessimism—so it is impressed on us by admonition in the *Theaetetus*, by myth in the *Phaedrus*, by historical example in the *Charmides*.

I think a good deal of the puzzlement over Platonism is a result of our beginning with the "Platonic Idea." Our minds like narration and description, or argument about familiar practical decisions. The Pre-Socratics started with a description of the natural world—a "real" description and behind the scenes, to be sure, but in imaginable terms. We may try to put the textbook notion of the Platonic world into materially imaginable terms and we come up with the mythology of the two-story world. Socrates, and Plato's dialogues, started with practical argument, but they are sometimes interspersed with intimations of and implications from the theory of ideas or with frank myths stressing the soul and its vision of the ideas. I like to start by saying that Socrates and Plato took for granted the existence of body, of bodily things. So far as I know, no Greek ever got around to doubting this, and if Socrates and Plato had doubted it or denied it, they would have argued or proclaimed, for this would have been real originality. The existence of the soul was not an accepted Greek assurance, and Socrates and Plato did argue and proclaim it. Among the souls they thought of were pretty certainly gods and certainly God. Socrates and Plato did throw some stones at the senses (and I think they overdid this), but the "world of the senses" or "sense world" with which they found fault was quite honestly sense acquaintance and not the things of which the senses are telling us. Those things change their characters, but they have characters; and our minds fix upon these characters, drop off the now scientifically needless thing, thus endow communication with meanings and words, and have these unchanging "ideas" (which once we knew directly in the company of the gods) to analyze and build with in our true knowledge. The coin in my pocket came into being and will pass away; my good deed is attempted and fails; but the circle and virtue were and will be or rather just are. And the horse? Well, there was a time before little eohippus and there are doubtless horseless worlds; any horse that meets the definition of horse is as good a horse—although he may not be as good at running or pulling—as any horse on earth or any heavenly horse. There is a sense in which it may be said that the circle is in a world, though in that world there should be no circular things. I do not think this is so of the horse. Define "horse," and when you get tired of defining the components of your definition the ultimate simples will be Platonic "Ideas," for you. For any natural species, among those components will be, in all probability, existence and existence "in nature." Is existence an idea? This is a verbal question and more than a verbal question. It is a question connected with the difficulty which the theory of ideas does raise for the problem of substance. It is not that Socrates and Plato deny body or bodily things. They do proclaim soul and idea. Is the soul substance? Is idea? Is matter? Or is some combination? This is indeed the background of the way in which Aristotle sometimes makes trouble, or seems to, for himself and his readers.

Socrates and Plato found in their "Ideas" a solution, an adjustment, and a fresh start for much of the exploring of the Pre-Socratics. In their enthusiasm for the "Idea" and the soul, they incited the natural tendency to give ontological separateness to the results of analytic insight and imagination. Aristotle is the Academic who counters the tendency and tries to keep the distinctions while reintegrating the being of idea and thing, of soul and living animal, or, more generally in his own doctrine, of form and matter.

On the other hand, the modern meaning for idea—a psychological existent, an "image," "in" the mind, a subjective presentation that may come from or be caused by the world but itself is a portion of consciousness not of what is out there—this new ontologic item may be just coming to be in Aristotle. It is certainly not general or accepted or express in Aristotle but can be felt as difficulties pile up in the *De anima*. There were, of course, as there are, many motives and scraps of belief in mental content: the behind-the-scenes scientism of Anaximander, the elevation of the numbers above the heard music of Pythagoras, the relativism of sense in Heraclitus, the call (possible) for illusion in Parmenides, the little simulacra of the atomists going from the object into the percipient (even though these are stanchly material), the complaints of the unstayingness of the world our senses tell us of as against the dependability of the ideational world of thinking in Plato. And for everyone there were dreams, ghosts, remembrances, imaginings. Aristotle gives a physiological accounting for dreams, with only an interpretable suggestion of mental content. It is probably true to say that appearance as a mental rubric, and especially as a philosophic puzzle over against reality, comes in connection with everyday perception and is only then easily and happily made use of to explain memory, fancy, dreaming, perhaps ghosts.

With the Greeks, even with Plato, the philosophic puzzle was apt to be given as "the one and the many." But with and after Plato, especially after the myth of the cave in the seventh book of the *Republic*, we hear more and more of the problem of appearance and reality. I think this has been a mistake. The proper contrary for reality is not appearance but something like contrivance. "One thing only I have found: God hath made man upright, but he hath made many contrivances."

I have become convinced that it is easiest, and true, to say there just are no appearances. There are appearings, as of the man who walks into the room where we are, as opposed to the nonappearing of the man who stays downstairs. But the man who came in is not an appearance any more than the man who did not come in is a nonappearance. It is, of course, linguistically familiar and proper to use the noun "appearance" for the fact of the man's coming into a place where there is someone who notes his coming. But this has been no part of the philosophers' depth. And there are ways of appearing, as of the man who stands with his right profile toward us as opposed to the way he could have stood, but does not, with his left profile toward us. Relations set subtle problems, and the relativity of secondary relations like right-and-left may well be of interest to the philosopher in his diving for reality through appearance, but it is not the topic of that problem. If there are only appearings (not appearances), then the problem of appearance and reality would seem to be merely the question of what at any time and place is actual, or beyond this of the difference of true and false belief as to what is appearing at other times and places or even here and now; and all this is reporting or history or the theory of fidelity in description or the technique of observation. If there are no appearances —and so, properly, still more no appearance—then the philosophers' long toil over appearance and reality seems a bit silly.

Yet it is certainly silly to say all these good minds and this good effort were silly. The problem is real if the formulation is mistaken. Shall we say the formulation appears to be mistaken? Or that its appearance to many philosophers as profound, basic, accurate was an "illusory appearance"? Surely there have been badly put problems (although probably never an altogether meaningless one). The putting of the problem seemed right, but the seeming is better not called an appearance. The putting was done by the mind, and the accepting was by the mind; it was not dropped in or around or before the mind like the veil of Maya or the shadows on the wall of Plato's cave or even like the "simple ideas" of John Locke. Here too we bow to the master idol (itself surely no simple or compounded content) that whatever we are thinking must be mental content, that there is nothing we use, or believe that we have made, more or less inexpertly, which we have contrived.

I want a substitute for appearance in the old opposition between reality and its rival; and I think it is, in some sense, contrivance. What has the mind made up, and to some extent believed and so embroidered on what appears, that is on what is really there as it appears? What would disappear, what would no longer be there, if my mind, or our minds, or all minds, were to not-be—or even to not-have-been? I think 2 plus 2 equals 4 is real, not contrivance; but not really there, not substantial. So odd and even numbers are real, although the "classes" of odd and even numbers may be a contrivance. A particular mathematician's preference for "intuitionist" or "formalist" or "logicist" theory of the nature of mathematics is a contrivance, as is the theory of the nature of mathematics, as is the class of mathematicians, as indeed is the natural species man. I think the man with a name who is an intuitionist mathematician is no contrivance but is real and also really there, a substance. So plurally are the many substances who are men and are mathematicians. And when I talk with one of them, I am talking with a substance who is talking about real nonsubstances and who is a member of an indefinite number of contrived classes and believes a large number of justified and unjustified, express and implicit, learned and popular theories and "facts."

The notion of substance here is Aristotle's. It is as he states it in the *Categories*. "Substance in the truest sense is something like this man, or this horse." It is that which may, which normally does, appear as the subject of a sentence but which cannot be predicated of a subject; nor can it be "present to a subject" (as a "certain point of grammar" may be present to a mind), although possibly it may be a part of a subject. Its truest characteristic is its hospitality for contrary predicates in time: substance, and only substance, changes.

Aristotle generally and this crabbed and splendid little work, the first in the *Organon*, especially, have been quarreled with as based on grammar; it has become the fashion to talk easily and with superiority of "subject-predicate" logic and of Greek and English idiosyncrasies. The points criticized sometimes seem far from anything I can find Aristotle saying; but beyond details I am willing to find the sensitivity of actual people in their actual dealings with—not thinking about—the pulling and pushing of existence: I am willing to find the linguistic deposit of those dealings a most hopeful clue to the natures and interrelations of those things people have been dealing with. And it is hard for me, on the basis of a not-large but some acquaintance with a number of languages, to imagine anyone who does not have some way of addressing his mate and of characterizing a thing's use or quality. To be sure, the move from Greek to English makes some troubles but also suggestively puts us on our guard; and the manifold and radical analogies of the uses of two languages which are as different as Greek and English are impressive. Of course the argument here is given differently elsewhere; although here put in grammatical terms, it can stand on other grounds, like Aristotle's biological teaching, which also sometimes appeals to language.

Thus we have the personal pronoun, the proper name, the demonstrative—the true substantive as pointing out, referring to a substance, what we can address, summon, applaud, chide, say something about in word as well as deal with, knock down, caress, run after, or run away from in our own substantiality. And we have the adjectival words, including verbs and prepositions as well as adjectives, still to be distinguished but all saying "something" which is never a "thing" about the substantial things.

A trouble Aristotle gets into in the first two or three pages of the *Categories* is that if we take position in the subject of a sentence as mark, we presently come to common nouns, class words, which cannot name "prime substances" since they also appear easily in the predicate (some as "secondary substances," all the species and genera. They are indeed the most important of the many mugwumps of discourse and theory—"with their mugs on one side of the fence and their wumps on the other" (Woodrow Wilson's one undignified campaign favorite). The common noun, if it be of a natural species, always carries its bodily substantial reference (denoting the things to which it points), but its meaning (denoting the character it requires to be in those things) is unsubstantial, from the predicative side. The more we think rather than deal, the more we resort to the common noun, the more we "generalize"—to a zone beyond which the common noun too, with its remnant but direct freightage of the world of material things, vanishes.

Aristotle loved the common noun; not only as the world's greatest observer and classifier of natural sorts but also as the master teacher of the teachers of predicative and syllogistic logic. Even with the mugwump "S" as "all or some S's" and "P" as "all or some P's," conversion is full of tricks; but it is passable for schoolroom manipulation. And Aristotle is more astute and wary than most of the later manipulators. Modern logic, having gone beyond, is ill at ease with the common noun and the copula, which it tries to forget by burying it. There seems to me, for all its care and elaboration, something insufferably artificial and complicated about the "quantification algebra." But symbolic logic has gone beyond, as developed science has gone beyond, the common noun. Thinking goes from the individual to the general to the universal and the formal. Time-space and point coordinates and mass numbers keep, for many surely, a tinge of reference to actuality; and so may logical constants and variables whether propositional or predicative. But it is a tinge for our substantial minds, and minimal.

Aristotle's difficulty is also shown in the *Categories* by the quickness with which, having pointed out that the substance cannot be predicated, he heads his list of the sorts of predicates with the "category of substance." Aristotle's point is that when we say "This is a dog," we are telling what sort of substance this is; but the predicate itself is also saying that the subject is a substance. To be sure any subject, if it be a "true" subject, is substantial. But when we say "The dog is brown," the predicate "brown" does not itself assert any individual substance; and we can, with an abstract subject, say "Tan is brown." This is typically Aristotelian in its sagacity and a sort of sagacious highhandedness toward theoretical impediments; but it is not altogether satisfactory. It makes the magisterial categories not on one level: the other categories after the "category of substance" are purely, or more purely, predicative. Whether we ought to say that a predicate term can at the same time predicate a predicative character of the subject and predicate that the subject is more than a predicative character because it is a substance; or whether we should phrase it differently so as to avoid talking of predicating nonpredicability is, I take it, mainly a verbal question. "Unpredicable" is, of course, a predicate, and when one—when Aristotle—says substance cannot be predicated, he is saying substance is unpredicable and is predicating nonpredicability of substance. More accurately, he says a substance cannot be a predicate (we may identify an individual with himself—"this dog is this dog"—but this is not proper predication). Thus we can say that substance is substantial; we can say that a dog is a substance; we can identify this dog as this dog; but we cannot take this dog or the words "this dog" and predicate it of any subject in the way in which we predicate big, black, sleeping, lying. The problem is then as follows: Aristotle says a substance cannot be predicated of a subject. Aristotle says the categories are a classification of predicates. Aristotle gives us as the first and chiefest of the categories the category of substance. We have a common noun like "dog," which easily and often appears as predicate. "The hound of the Baskervilles was indeed a dog." When we say that sentence, we are saying what sort of thing the subject is, but in so saying we are also asserting that the subject is a thing, a substance. We are predicating substantiality of a substance as well as predicating a kind, a form; our natural species, our true common nouns, are made for this purpose, are contrived mugwumps. But they do not, because they cannot, predicate any actual substance, any "this substance here," of anything, because this is a sub-

stance and it cannot be, and its name cannot be, a predicate.
A predicate is a "universal," which is "predicable of many
things," whereas an individual is, and is itself, and may be a
part, and may even be a thing having parts, but cannot be
predicated of anything—as Aristotle also tells us briefly and
emphatically in De Interpretatione, chapter VII, and right
at the end of the Posterior Analytics.

Aristotle does not tell us all this. He just observes that
a substance cannot be predicated, that the categories are
highest sorts of predicates, that the first category is the category of substance. But I do not think he would object to
my schoolteacherish transition and explanation. He hints it
in the summarization of the doctrine of the categories in
Book I, 9 of the Topics.

In that little chapter of the Topics also appears, especially in the different translations of the Categories and the
Topics in the Oxford Aristotle, one of the root difficulties
in the tradition stemming from Aristotle—as to substance,
the partial rivalry of "essence" with "substance" for the
Greek "οὐσία." I believe it is in the Categories, according
to the usual dating of Aristotle's works, that he introduced
the word "οὐσία" for substance and laid down the doctrine
of substance as "like this man or this horse" to which, despite
many sideline and historical arguings, he always came back.
I say he introduced "οὐσία" for "substance" with frank
anachronism. He points out that to which it refers and the
characteristic marks by which its reference can be identified;
but, like most introducers of words, he does not expound
why he picked the word. It is a form of the Greek verb "to
be" and seems decidedly better than the Latin-English "substance"—the "sub" and "stare" ("standing under") have led
to easy misdirection. Aristotle used two other forms of the
verb "to be," "τί ἐστι" and "τὸ τί ἦν εἶναι," in a similar ab-
stract-noun-sense. Most careful scholarship is now apt to use

"substance" for "*οὐσία*" and "essence" for "*τί ἐστι*" and *τὸ τί ἦν εἶναι*"; but many translators will use still other expressions for either, depending upon their understanding of what is being said.

Certainly, when it is clearest in Aristotle, substance is the existent thing and essence is the definition, the combination of characters which makes something a member of the species defined. The reference of the species is to a collection (usually an uncollected collection) of existent things, each of which has those defining characters, both that essence (along with many other, "accidental," characters) and that sheer existence, that substantiality, which is not normally expressed in the definition and so is not "of the essence," although, if we know that the species is a natural species, we may know that existence of its members is asserted in the species name, the common noun, even if not at all in the definition. Essence is logical—is logic; substance is existential—is existent. There may be significance in the defect of precise analogy between logical-logic and existential-existent-existence. In the *Topics* chapter Aristotle says: "For when a man is set before him and he says what is set there is 'a man' or 'an animal,' he states the essence and signifies a substance; but when a white color is set before him, he says that what is set there is 'white' or is 'a color,' he states its essence and signifies a quality." Essence is stated; substance is. Substance, simply, is not stated, is not predicated, even when the reference of the "secondary substance" common noun is essentially to a substance or substances. For the essentiality of the reference to substance is in the semantic character of the word as a natural common noun, not in the essence which its meaning carries. If we use or hear "a cat" or "cats" and we know the language, we know we are talking of things in the world (substance) and that the sort of things we are talking about are sleek, agile, and meowing things (essence). In the *Metaphysics* (Zeta [vii], 4;1030a5), Aristotle says: "Individuality belongs only to substances. Therefore there is an essence only of those things whose formula is a definition." And the individual has no definition.

I am aware that this distinction, which is uncomfortably close for many to the "connotation and denotation" with which they struggled, has been fashionably high-hatted in these generations and that a number of acute attempts have been made to reduce one side to the other. The acuteness seems to me singularly unperceptive, and I should be willing to argue; but it might certainly be that I am wrong. My concern here is with Aristotle. For him the distinction, and difference, is important (and he offers it, for those willing to be helped to understand, as a key to the preceding "theory of ideas" of Socrates and Plato), and it is necessary not only to interpreting Aristotle but to getting along with the later divagations of "substance" and "essence." And we do that "majestical" spirit "wrong" [1] if we snub him as a mere expounder of "subject-predicate grammar" or as not an expounder of a formalized "meta-grammar."

The central importance of Aristotle may be his ability (imperfect as all abilities are imperfect) to accept, find, create, keep distinctions in theory, while rejecting or being suspicious of separateness or even separability in the world of things. Theory is analytic and synthetic; substance is integral.

1. Shakespeare's language does not quite fit: "majesty" is a post-Roman encomium, not Greek, or Aristotelian. Incidentally, it was a Roman-admirer and Medieval who called Aristotle "the master of those who know," which is fair enough except that he is still the follower of Socrates who knew he did not know and was wary of being the master of those who thought they knew. I should rather call Aristotle the sagacious master of those who are curious, and curious not so much to know as to understand.

The distinction between thing and character, subject and predicate, noun and adjective or verb, topic and assertion, individual and general or particular, the individual and the universal, logic and existence, theory and the actual, substance and mode is in all probability the greatest discovery in basic theory, in metaphysics and logic. It was made, or made sufficiently clear, by Socrates, or, if you prefer, by Plato. The first way of putting the distinction, thing and character, is the basic one, is itself in the real world in the sense that we deal with things and think of them as things with characters. The distinction is not perfectly expressed, but I doubt if you can find another word for thing as good as "thing." "Character" is less good and can be variously replaced, as with "characteristic." The last pair, "substance and mode," is also intentionally in the real world but is more learned. The problematic meaning of "substance" is the center of our problems. My willingness to take it as saying "thing" is perhaps the most helpful thing (which of course is not a thing) I can say in regard to my answer, to the problem, and Aristotle's answer. "Mode" in its historic usage is too narrow and suggestive to do the job here, but I think of no better substitute. The other listed pairs come rather from our linguistic and logical usage in our ways of expressing the two distinguished items than from the actuals themselves. Perhaps for that reason they may be especially helpful; and their use we owe to Aristotle and his logical acumen.

The linguistic and grammatical path that Aristotle liked, along with his factual and especially biological interest, helped keep him from going along with the taking of distinction as separation, especially from going along with the separateness of thing and character, thing and "Idea," to which the enthusiasm of discovery pressed Socrates and Plato. We know that adjectives of shape and of color are distinct genera of adjectives, of predicates, of character; we even know we can study geometry and can study color in a variety of scientific and pragmatic ways without bothering about the color of the shape or the shape of the color. We can come close to seeing a shapeless color or colors in the atmosphere, but ordinarily we see colored shapes or shaped colors or, indeed, in the actual world we do not see, and our grammar tells us we do not see, either colored shapes or shaped colors but things that have both shape and color. There are ways, and must be ways, in which adjectival ideas can be applied to other adjectival ideas; but in normal sentences—assertions about the world around us and with us—the subject is not an adjective but a substantive; we are talking about a substance not a character. The things move about independently, except for external relations with some other things.

Yet it is also true that the all-considering Aristotle flirts with the separability of these distinctions, which he does not want to separate, and so flirts with the parceling out of being, and so of οὐσία, substance, among them. The *Metaphysics* is an intricate struggle with such seductions, a struggle that yet never succumbs to them. One motive bending Aristotle to flirtation can be noted in what we called the unsatisfactory nature of the word "character" as the opposite partner of "thing." For most of us, "character" either has a substantial suggestion (as when we speak of a person having a "strong character" in much the same way he might have a heavy coat) or—even when it is used of what is quite adjectival—it has a static suggestion as of a visible state which the eye can, as it likes to, fix into an unchanging picture. (We are most of us visualists.) Now it is true that the character, the predicate, the idea, is abstract from existential change and to this dependability owes its ability to enable discourse—we need this dependability even to talk to ourselves—but now, added to the fact that a predicate does not change its meaning, we have the assertion that it means that which does not change. The word "change" itself may tell the story. The "change" that Virgil deplored is the same that is today deplored or hailed; but that thing of which change is truly asserted must be changing all the time the assertion is true. "Time and chance are busy ever." "Busy" is an adjective that does not allow static representation or reference. If we take our meanings as unchanging in both ways, then we may be eased into trying to account for the changing world with two unchanging components: an unchanging stuff which (mysteriously) takes on, instances, a succession of unchanging characters. For Aristotle the word "predicate" seems to have tended to take this double logical changelessness. So in the precious paragraph of his fundamental doctrine of substance, in the *Categories*, where he is emphasizing the fact that substances change as their most sure mark, he finds himself stating that substances are able to have contrary predicates at different times. Doubtless Martha, the substance who was "busy about many things," had different, "contrary," predicates as she took her busyness from the kitchen to the dining room, but her busyness itself is enough to affirm that she was not being a mathematical identity during any of the time she was busy.

I am not forgetting that my or our feeling about "character" need not have been Aristotle's, that indeed he used Greek. The word we translate as "predicate," the noun, comes, I am told, from the verb "κατηγορέω" from the lingo of the auctioneer and the herald. Thus the frequent way of saying "thing," that "thing" which our antisubstantialists say substantialists have "reified" out of the unchanging substance which is "under" the changes, is πράγμα, something being done or going on. These process suggestions of the word's etymology seem fairly soon lost. It is the tendency of our reflected sensing to turn to images and of our thinking to think of the steady meanings of our terms of discourse. This is not a radical inadequacy or vice of our senses or our thinking. Seeing, especially, is at fault; and yet seeing is subtle and lively in the perception of qualitative change; and thinking is the great, if not the only, "time binder." But we look for what is memorable and store it as pictures, and in time-binding we get bemused by our wrapping, string, and labels. Remembering that we live through, that we see "God make himself a mighty rose of dawn," and that there is no change for which we cannot make an unchanging word and meaning, we do not have to become anti-intellectualists to escape "intellectualism."

Aristotle has another motive for flirting with the separation of distinguishable aspects and the assignment of some οὐσία among them before returning, as he always does, to his first love of substance in "the first and truest sense" as "this man or this horse." This motive for the great classifier is in the lack of levelness of the items being distinguished. The Platonists view the sense thing and the "Idea" as two different beings, each somehow making faces at the other. If this is a caricature, it is Aristotle's—who yet was an academic. But also for Aristotle the character, the "form," is not a thing; it exists only in the thing. When abstracted and thought, it is free and naked of existent concreteness. But the thing is always meant as existing, and as existing is characterized, multiply and with "accidental" characters as well as with "essential" ones. The distinction is between what is always a whole and what is essentially a part (in some sense) of such a whole. We can and should think the character apart from the thing, any thing, but we cannot think the thing apart from some such characters; we are thinking the character abstracted from existence, but we must not think a thing abstractly except as we think of a sort of things—a half or mugwump abstraction—or as we may struggle to turn "thingness" into a character as that which is predicable of all things.

We like to keep our distinctions, our dilemmas and alternatives and species, on the same level—between one animal and another, one answer and another, one enemy or ally and another, one place to go on vacation and another, one girl and another. The great classifier, Aristotle, thinking of species of a genus, wants his species on a level and mutually exclusive. But thing and character are not species of a genus, are not on a level, and cannot be mutually exclusive since they, differently, imply one another and existentially involve one another. So Aristotle argues, weighs, qualifies, dismisses or allows "in a sense." And so, in brief, after Aristotle, for the most hurtful of the historic errors about substance, we come up with substance as the altogether unchanging component of a concrete thing, and character (or whatever) as all the changingness of a concrete thing.

If Aristotle is right, the real thing is not concrete. To make the stuff named "concrete" we put several separately existing materials into a big tank, revolve it, and pour out the soon-hardening amalgam, well mixed but literally put together. And this is a good instance of the adjective "concrete." In the process of abstraction, only the character has been abstracted, taken away; and the character that has been abstracted is in its nature abstract, not like the money the bank thief abstracts from the safe and can then spend in the world. The abstracted character can be used in theory, can be predicated and analyzed and admired in contemplation; but it will not move a feather on a table edge. What is the proper opposite for "abstract"? The "concrete" of the English composition teacher will not do here. The prefix "con" gives it away, as "con" and "com" do a lot of other words, as indicating the resultant of a putting together. We can, in a proper sense of the word, synthesize an abstraction with other abstractions in a complex notion or theory; we cannot synthesize abstractions in the chemists' sense of synthesizing vitamins. And we cannot synthesize, or concresce, or put together the abstraction, the abstracted character, with what is left after the abstracting and achieve a thing; we cannot put together the character and whatever in a thing is not character and have a thing. And if Aristotle is right, nature cannot do so either.

I do not think we should run away from the puzzles of what we mean by "real" or discard the criterion "real," at least until we have not only tried and failed to find but have also made plausible why no such meaning exists and yet everyone uses the word and the criterion. In one question with regard to wholes and parts there is a simple factual difference associated with relative reality which is sometimes easily known or determinable and still more often easily imaginable and understandable. Did the parts exist before they were put together in the whole? Did the whole exist before we could take the parts out of it? Must the whole exist before we can even imagine deriving the parts from it, so that the parts cannot exist separately? The word "artifacts" seems to mean that of artifacts the first question is to be answered yes. The parts of the clock were there, or were made, and then were assembled by the clockmaker. The voluntary association of individuals in a club or a firm, although not an artifact, seems safely composed of prior parts. There have been debates about priorities in the state and the family, but I should be an individualist about both, especially the state. There are separately existing stuffs that mix chemically, are not just assembled; but chemical analysis will suffice to rederive the components.

There are things of which the second question—Did the whole exist before we could take the parts out of it?—

may be answered yes; although there is more apt to be disagreement here. Some elements come only in association with others: smelting is among our oldest technologies and subatomic derivation among our newest. But these same elements might, I suppose, be differently given on other planets. There are unicellular organisms and a cell can be extracted from a biological body. Can the unicellulars be combined not only into a colony or population but also into an "individual" animal?; can a cell be made like the extracted cell, or in any case put together by external arrangement or grafting so as to make a cat like that from which a cell can be extracted? In speech many phones seem unviable except as part of at least a phoneme and quite absurd except as occurring in a used language. Even in classical mechanics the vectors into which a motion or force may be discomposed are meaningful of separate motions which could exist separately, but the actual motion which is being so analyzed was not itself put together of those components.

There are things of which the third question—Must the whole exist before we can even imagine deriving the parts from it, so that the parts cannot exist separately?—may be answered yes. Of these, the type is the soul. What are the parts of the soul? And if you object, as many will, to the word "soul," you may call it as you will; but if you object that "it" is not a "thing" and so falls outside our questions about substantial parts and wholes (that for Aristotle, most of the time, it is a "form" of the living thing not itself a thing), then you have a harder objection calling for more circumspection.

The whole clock is more interesting and important than the unassembled pieces (except as these intrigue the historian of the clock). This is the clock in its function, and its function is its action, one of Aristotle's categories beyond the category of substance; and the interest and use of the clock are its value (which Aristotle did not name as a category but which I should) and have their appeal to the action, to the wit and need, of a person—another substance. The function of the clock is, in Aristotle's language, only potentially in its parts—indeed only by a second potentiality since the whole clock has it only potentially when it is run down. So the function of this composite thing, the clock, is in the mechanically external relations of its makeup. Now to many the clock will seem, and with justice, to be more real than its parts. On the basis of existential separateness and antecedence, the parts are the more real. But for Aristotle the clock also is "prior" as that for which, as an end in view, the parts were devised, made, and put together. And an implication of this is a direct factor in our frequent use of "real" and "more real": the clock is what I am interested in, what is serviceable, what is "better," what "has more being." As to the association of animals in a pack, of humans in a firm or club or state, of states in a United Nations, of humans (or organisms) in a family, I remain an individualist here also. The function and interest are still in external relations, as in all the existent world, but these are now less simply mechanical and in the case of the family are in part biological, integral, and so, from the point of view of one who thinks the living has more being than the nonliving, are more substantial. The integralness of the way the parts of any organism are together in the whole seems in command, and I find myself on the "holistic" side. The animal is not put together of his parts, as is the clock; but, like the clock, is the "end" (if not "in view") which gives meaning and value to the parts. Yet I can understand and, knowing the good difference of interests, I can say as I said to a famous geneticist at lunch one day: "I think of the animal as more real than the cells; but I guess you think of the cells as more real." He smiled and said "Yes." Still the geneticist's interest in the cell is in mytosis and in chromosomes and DNA, and these develop into the adult. To be sure, we are adults and biased, but would even a disembodied intelligence be interested in the adult as the postlude to the genes as he might be interested in the genes as prologue to the adult? Or am I merely biased because Aristotle says the chicken must come before the egg, otherwise the egg would not know which way to go? In a temporal and literal sense an adult, or two adults, must work to bring about a new one and continue the species; but in a much more important sense the form must be logically prior to the material potentiality. It may be that there is no specific form ahead of the moving particle in time because it is already in timelessness. But, Aristotle says, "Matter yearns for form as the female yearns for the male" (with typical Greek male snootiness). Without the assured betterness of adding (the right) form, the possibility of greater reality, there would not be even blind "yearning," aspiration.

The radical opposing position, or a radical opposing position, looks back to the clock and uses the clockmaker's analogy not in eighteenth-century fashion in the interest of natural religion but for Democritean materialism. Some scientists still hold to the old-fashioned "scientific continuity" and have faith that when we know more we can make biology and psychology as mechanical as mechanics without leaving all the dramatic world of meanings and values not only absurd in its content but inexplicable in its occurrence as illusion. Life and soul will then be not an Aristotelian form, as the "first entelechy of a body having life naturally within it," but, as Aristotle says soul is for Democritus, the shape of the arrangement of the atoms in the void. The unity of the person, of the animal, of the thing, becomes a matter of degree and unimportant but simply enough determinable insofar as present at all in the togetherness with which a group of atoms moves. Thus, unless special rules of internal motion are adopted, the animal will have less individuality than the crystal. Materialism has its very great attractions; but most of the time I would rather go back to Thales and deny that there is any pure matter if matter is to be defined as lifeless.

I have been saying, long-windedly, that Aristotle's substance is integral, not abstract and as surely not concrete as put together. The prime substance "in the truest sense" is a thing like this horse or this man. This horse cannot be defined; but he has characters, especially reproductive characters that enable him to keep his species in existence, that make him a member of his natural species and of many others under the category of substance. He is bodily but he is not put together of body and characters. He has parts but he is not put together of his parts. He is an "ensouled body" as Aristotle called him or, as Socrates might have suggested, an embodied soul; but both phrases are too compositional to be accurate. He is "himself, a simple separate person," yet not simple as a number is simple and, if separate, always in interaction. Leibniz was right: the point and the particle are beautiful and useful; but the point is not there, and the particle is just a step in either dissection or abstraction. The thing endures.

Substance is things. Aristotle says, I think acceptably even against the modern fear of being anthropocentric, that a man is "higher" than an animal because in addition to the animal's sensitive soul he has a rational soul, just as the animal is higher than the plant because in addition to the plant's nutritive soul, which man also has, he has a sensitive soul, and the plant is higher than the inorganic thing because the plant has soul. A man is a fool if he does not feed himself and reproduce, if he does not move about in pursuit of food and pleasure; but he is especially blamable if he is not curious and trying to understand. For my part I think that aspiration and weariness, integral to all response and effort, are as wide as life; and with my tendency toward Thales I am willing to think there is no altogether lifeless thing, no unsouled thing. But even in that extremity the gradations of consciousness such as Aristotle used are necessary. They help with the difficulties we got into with the clock and with the criterion of relative independence in respect of smaller parts and larger collections. Most of the time I am willing to be hospitable to "mere" things. They move about as more or less dependable units, have their relative independencies; some are beautifully structured, like the crystals; some are structured for the interest and use of humans, like the clock. Organisms add their own integration, the unity, individuality, of a point of view. It is proper, not surprising or reprehensible, that a theory like Aristotle's—which seeks substance in the integral, in that which is really there to be explained and not in the end products of the abstraction or dissection of explanation—that such a theory should be willing to use more than one mark of what thing is a thing. There are things that are bodily firm against the supposition that they are just aspects or embroideries of things our minds have contrived. There are still more surely substantial things whose psychic individuality is assurance that they are not just parts or collections of other things. There are also clearly unclearnesses and difficulties (what shall we say of time and space?), and our knowledge of even the elements of substantialism is deficient.

One of the first things I learned from a bookmaker was (that gamblers are honest and) that if you cannot win you cannot lose. (I bet a horse to show; he ran fourth; I went in to pay; the bookmaker said that particular horse had been "out to show" and it was no bet; I kept my money, properly, although I had been wrong in my judgment.) Implied in that is that if you cannot lose you cannot win. Substance is a gambler. A person may want to be a dishonest gambler or even not to gamble, but substantially he is part of an existent world and he is gambling. It is thus we say substance endures, as mathematics does not and as the coloring of the sunset does not. Do not look for something for nothing? Every moment the future, which was not at all, comes from the present, which then is not, and comes more or less largely for nothing, as the result of no payment. Through that, substance endures; and the "higher" the substance, the more it loses and wins. So if substance is a gambler, again the man is more substance than the rock. Virtue, I shall say, does come for something, but it is probably more apt to come to one who has known losses. How else should it be its own reward? And surely no gambler wants to think he is just an observer of a causeless succession of phenomena or even events. Chance there is, I believe; but our dependable ignorance of antecedent and circumstance will guarantee luck, good or bad, for us. And freedom there is, I am still more sure. But cause there is, too, the Greek ἀνάγκη, operating in and by substance as all that endures in a world of eternal numbers and shifting relations; and the gambler has a right to pat himself on the back for his judgment and management as well as the need to say thanks for the luck.

Since Aristotle if not since Adam we think of things largely with common nouns, and common nouns mean classification (and we called Aristotle the great classifier). One of the persistent undertones of his thinking—and even more one of the persistent if misunderstood themes of his influence—was the notion of a completed classification, never made but ideally there. Curiously Aristotle never expounded his theory of classification.[2] Perhaps it had been stock-in-

2. Bits of it exist in the *Posterior Analytics* and elsewhere; more in *Parts of Animals*, chap. 1, one of the better summaries of Aristotelian elements.

trade in the Academy, and he just assumed his students would know it. We, too, teach a little about it in high school and then take it for granted. The fact is, I think, that no one yet has seen through it and made what he saw clear. We can say that the plural of "species" is "species" and of "genus" is "genera"; we can note that the species "puts a face" on the genus as specie does with bullion; we can require that the species of a genus be exclusive and exhaustive and that the differentiae be of a kind; and we can be comfortable in the middle ranks of at least some classifications. But where does the ideal completed classification end as it goes down, as it goes up, as it spreads out?; where do we get the differentiae?; if it is complete, could we have another? Philosophy has been defined as a criticism of the categories (not a bad cocktail-party answer), and what we need to know for this is all about how cats and elephants are quadrupeds and mammals; triangles are equilateral, isosceles, or scalene; magenta and solferino are red; submarines and frogmen are divers—or are they?; being is not a genus; you cannot be defined.

The important point for us would seem to be that although things are that for the sake of which classification is made—"we classify things" primarily—one peers in vain into any classification for a thing. None is there, for a classification is a set of classes, or class words, and a thing is not a class. It is our familiar contrariety of logic and existence, abstraction and substance. Below the line under the lowest biological species we choose to differentiate are the actual individual proper-name cats and elephants. It is true now, as we compare the category of substance with the other categories, that our common nouns under substance are never pure logic because they always retain reference to actual existent things and, by the same token, that it becomes questionable whether under the other categories there is a "line" and whether there are individual or particular instances under that line if there be one. Mr. Fisher's racing silks were put down on the program as solferino; but racing silks are already classified somewhere under the substantial listing, and if they are now called into use under the category of quality, they will be duplicated. It also seems those silks may be individuals or themselves classes; and the choice looks arbitrary. Aristotle's ten, nine, or eight categories have seemed too many to most since his time. For years I got along, awkwardly but sufficiently, with four: substance, action, quality, relation; until I became acutely aware that I needed value. But with value I see I need two up-and-down lines: one between substance and all the others and one between value and all the preceding, since value has meaning only after the characters to the left are actual. Even within the central group of three categories there are curious failures of symmetry. Action more closely involves substance, yet relation, nearer the mathematical "intermediates" as Aristotle apparently called them, is better able to stand alone as enabling a formal system. For all their reverend beauty and their place as keys to a classification that is all a system of species and genera, the categories themselves hardly seem species of any genus and hardly seem genera of the species below.

Putting aside these and other charming riddles, I want to say that when I imagine a perfect observer who without any "idols" or embroideries of his own or humanity's should simply perceive what is there, I think he would perceive a world of things and not a classification. Let us chart the world of what is really there as a square enclosing each thing; that imposing triangle or pyramid of classification which many minds have thought of since Aristotle would be off to the side, partly imbedded in the square of substance since the characters on the basis of which men have recognized or set up the classes are, basically, actually there in the actual things.

Off to the other side of the square, even more deeply imbedded, I should say, but still detachable, will be the maps —the neat elimination and construction we call mapping, a procedure sometimes mixed with and sometimes confused with classification. (The *Sunpapers'* famous cartoonist Yardley, when drawing a map of Maryland, will show a crab coming up out of Chesapeake waves and a pretty milkmaid in the fields of Frederick County.)

There are two more additions which we will chart above and below our square of substances, also partly imbedded in it: the parts actually to be found within the things and the collections in which the things figure as parts. When we map we attend to certain features, say roads, perhaps regularize them, and ignore the rest or most of the rest of the actuality. Thus the map is like the part, but it is abstractive rather than dissective as is the discovery of parts, whether the dissection be actual or suppositive: the network of roads is a formalized picture of one aspect of the picture of the countryside; the brick in the wall, the salt in the omelette is constitutive.

The collection is like the class. Indeed the two have been identified more frequently, and for some engineering or set-theory purposes there is advantage in treating them together. But here, too, the two sorts of "sets" differ ontologically, and the processes of making and recognizing them differ as dissection and abstraction, in this case aggregation and generalization. An actual collection has to be tied together by proper name, demonstrative, time and place: the crabs now in Chesapeake Bay, the chairs in this room, the horses in the first race run in 1968, the trio Julius Caesar, the General Motors Corporation, and Rudolph the Reindeer. The class is tied together by a definition, and a definition is by definition open.

It may be noted that I consider the characters of things as real, really of the real things within the square of substance; whereas the classes and classification set up on the basis of those characters and their associations in existent things, being noted and chosen and partly made by the mind, I find to be contrivances. Thus, despite my unwillingness to identify logical species, even the natural ones, with actual collections, I am not a "realist" with respect to class words, class ideas, or classes.

Parts, collections, maps, classifications are contrivances, not reality. But they are first and imbedded contrivances. They comprise, select, compound, tell literal truth of substances. There are, of course, badly made contrivances, all or partly false: assertions of phlogiston in burning bodies, of a plot by the Elders of Zion, maps that lead us astray, definitions that, perhaps intentionally, turn out to be contradictory. But the higher ranges of contrivance, with its glories, its stupidities, foibles, and promises, lie beyond. Our faultless observer will see all events as they happen; but history is in the books and remembrances of humans, and while he sees books and humans he does not see their intentionalities. Explanation, hypothesis, theory, natural law and science, since they are contrived, will not be given him; and if he wants them, he will have to make them for himself or return into the discourse of humans and become a student. Myths—the imagined stories that, especially after they become familiar, explain un-understood or misunderstood facts as presented—are good or bad artistry which may even turn out to be true: Santayana speaks of the "charming myths of Plato and Aristotle which no one will be the worse for knowing and few will be the worse for believing." Of course the ascriber of "myth" may be mistaken. What is the meaning of "symbol" and "symbolic," and what items are symbol or literal? I have heard Professor Alsoph Corwin tell of the variously tinged surprise when the electron microscope showed organic chemists that the carbon molecule actually looks like the pretty many-colored models they had trained themselves to call "mere models."

Formal science, mathematics and logic, is a problem of its own. I have said that our faultless observer will see the characters of things as they are, and so he will observe their changes and doings, their qualities, their relations. At least all actualized "Ideas" will be before him. And I have put myself on the side of Pythagoras and Socrates to agree that these Pythagorean numbers and Platonic "Ideas" are real. But they are not "there," they are not existent, except as some substantial thing presents some of them for one moment or many to our minds in the interaction of things or perhaps stirs our minds to recollection of them in their timeless aspect. Surely mathematics is the queen of contrivances (and it is the story of its discovery and elaboration and creation that I missed when I studied mathematics in school—my children fared better—and which I found only when I came back to it through the study of the history of philosophy). Mathematics is contrivance, but a contrivance with eternal and intuited materials.

Are there dreams? Undeniably there are dreamings. There are subjectivities of all shadings and gradations: from imaginings of the actual but not present, to "kisses feigned on lips that are for others," after-images, hot flashes, hunger for any food, hunger for fame, panic, fear, dull boredom, cruelty, amusement, creature comfort—doings and sufferings and yet with a seeming, a content or datum seeming which normally is not an "appearance" of anything. I do not suppose these will be observed by our faultless observer. Indeed they are not observed by the person who has them, although he may be more aware of them than of any observable. I shall call them, provisionally and with some apology, contrivance, but in origin a pre-intellectual contriving of the interacting substances, learned in feeling and crawling and falling and jumping, and later multiplied and richly embroidered from our life of observing and explaining.

When I think of substance this year I am apt to think of the "Big Trees" in California, the *Sequoia gigantea* of the High Sierra. For many years I have wanted to see them (in our more-than sense of "see"); I have often said they were the one thing I was sure of positively hoping to see; and this summer I was with them a while. In these redwoods we have something imposingly substantial. I think I am more substantial along a real dimension. I have more of the knowing and choice that make individuality. My mere getting there I could stake briefly against their being there. I knew it would not be easy for a nonmotorist from Maryland, but I did not guess how much hardihood, fortitude, and ingenuity would be needed. So I took a measure of self-congratulation out among the trees; but my human ability to admire and be humbled is much more. The Big Trees' hardihood and fortitude is real and superbly successful. What can match them? "This tree was born," says the central tag on the cross-section of a fallen tree in the Giant Forest, as I recall it, "in 465 B.C." I know it was a few years from Socrates in 469. That marvel of Athenian hardihood and fortitude has been gone 2,300 years. "This tree fell in 1955," says the outermost tag.

And the tree's hardihood, if simpler, is living, as is the man's. No one could tell me how to get to Sequoia National Park—in Baltimore, in Honolulu, in San Francisco, even in Fresno, just downstairs from Sequoia in the San Joaquin Valley. Not a few could tell me, it seemed, how to get to Yosemite, and some were quick to tell me, if I had not seen Yosemite, that that of course was what I wanted to see. I do not doubt the beauty of Yosemite (and the dizziness—the famous road up to Sequoia was too dizzying for me). But the falls and the peaks are not the substances the trees are. They are substance; and as a group they are older than the trees, young as the Sierra Nevada is among mountain ranges. Yet if alive at all, they are much less alive. And so their changes are externally imposed and their endurance is material. "Fortitude" seems misapplied and their hardihood, magnificent, is passive. The trees of the Sierra have something even of my ingenuity. Each tree has chosen from year to year, not merely fed itself and pushed but pushed here and there as it found its situation and found solution. I think they do not differ as severally as our Maryland oaks; but they are perceptibly individual, each in its situation and yet also differing as an individual even from its twin or triplet, when it is one of those frequently growing right together in a line. The crag, the river resisted, was worn, was changed, did not peer or try or reach. The mountains are substantial, but less so than the trees, and only with some arbitrariness of separation as substances. A larger proportion of the mountains than of the trees have been given names; but the trees wear their names with a difference. Aristotle would have agreed.

One early and lingering ailment of classification, which afflicted Aristotle once in awhile but which he vigorously countered, and which much more has afflicted some who came afterward in the influence of the Aristotelian picture of a completed classification, has come from the fact that we write from the top of the page down. Platonic "division," as in the *Sophist*, began with the wide sort and worked down toward the few they were "trying to catch" (although that quarry had to be kept in mind from the start). And classification keeps the arrangement on the page and indeed adds the notion that nature specifies the genus into the species. Just as the knowledge of the downward goal is needful in division, so the upward goal and the logic of the system are needful in classification, although modern statements of the process and Aristotle's own biological practice work from individuals to a class and so on up. At any rate by firm tradition, if not by the requirement of writing without smearing what has been written, the "summum genus" is at the top and the "infimae species" are at the bottom, and the individuals, if reckoned apart from the lowest species (as importantly they should be but not always were), are at the very bottom. So the more general is higher than the more specific, and the specific is higher than the individual. And the higher is the better.

My teacher Arthur Lovejoy used to say that a philosopher should never use the word "higher" because of this human linkage of "higher" and "better." I have already used the word in some difference-making ways: I have not followed his prohibition, but I respect his wariness. And I think the higher ranks in classification are further from substance, so in a sense are less real, and, since it is good to be real, they are, if anything, worse than the lower ranks. Much of this tradition of the betterness of the higher in classification as it is written is represented in the fondness of many, in different schools, for calling the scheme of classification a "hierarchy." The pyramidal shape in which it is written (or which the writing suggests—one cannot write a pyramid) does look like the way a hierarchy is written "down." And yet the difference seems almost amusingly clear. A hierarchy, etymologically and in usage still, is a chain of command or succession of widening ranks of command. How can a class command a class especially when the commanding class is made up of precisely the same members as the lower species over which it has command? It seems less a hierarchy than its opposite, the universe's biggest town meeting: all things command all component groups. The proper hierarchy is like that of which the pseudo-Dionysius the Areopagite tells us: cherubim, seraphim, archangels, and the rest of the nine orders; and so down to the hierarchies of churches; and so by extension to the United States Army; or the corporation for which you work.

Neoplatonism has sometimes seemed to me more properly Neoaristotelianism because of the looming of the classification pyramid in its structure. But Plotinus thought of himself as a Platonist, and a man has a right to set his own name. Also the figure of speech of the sun in the seventh book of the *Republic* is a more rhetorical support for the Plotinian hierarchy. Classification seems to me a combination of substantial things "below the line" and nonsubstantial classes making up the classification itself. The Neoplatonist, if he felt called on to justify his opposite and tiered substantialization of the pyramid, might repeat my radical ontological separation of the things and the class notions. He might remind me that Aristotle can be taken as saying (in different places) that the form is the formula, is the essence, is the definition of a sort, and that the soul is the form of the living thing. Now for the Neoplatonist, as for the Brahman, the separateness of existence is bad, a defect of being, and we can view the move across the line from our individuality to the definitions, essences, classes, as a move from the individuals, who have gone off and are going further off into matter, back up into a world of soul, or of Soul. And he might remind me that in my own interpretation of classification, if there are no more accepted ontological leaps, there is an un-understood thinning as we get to the categories and again as we try to go beyond the categories to the highest genus or some ultimate X of generality. The

Neoplatonist will welcome mysticism and the ineffable, but he is not going to accept anything un-understood. Why not see two more ontological lines across the ascending ranks: one as the differentiae lapse, into the realm of Spirit; and the other, as even the categories become too particular, into the absolute One. The One, like and much more than the sun, pours out its rays of being, out and down through Spirit and Soul and separate existences where the darkness of materiality and nonbeing separate and dilute the light. So we need to be converted, to turn from the darkness we seem to see with our senses and manipulate with our logic and mathematics, to make our way in being and in knowing back up the high path to the acme from which all being and knowing come.

In this doctrine, as in its contemporary congener Christian Science, the common-sense reader has trouble with a persistent refusal of distinctions, even distinctions of parts of speech, which Aristotle had loved and worked to clarify. The basis is shaken, in that the proper name and the personal pronoun have become somewhat illusory, the separate thing is suspect, and matter is no longer a stuff or substrate but a "false way of looking at things" that are not things. Substance is said to be truth, not that of which an existential statement presumes to be true. This is not a just reproach where distinction is an intrusion of nonbeing and where distinguishing is an attention of the separated mind to nonbeing rather than being, or at least to nonbeing as though it were in addition to being. The Neoplatonists themselves, notably Proclus, recognized that they could be called Neo-parmenidean; offering, however illogically (that is mystically), what Parmenides failed to provide: a doctrine of illusion.

Mysticism I am grateful to and susceptible to; but the doctrinal details that follow the announcement of the deceptiveness of words and the unspeakableness of reality seem to me myths in need of redress. Or perhaps it is mostly that I like my world of individual selves and common-sense things. Plotinus deserves his usual ranking as the greatest thinker between Aristotle and, at least, Augustine—700 years. His doctrine has attraction and its measure of truth. I think I could do better at making it my own than I could with modern subjective phenomenalism. This is in part because, its differences from me being more radical, they do not annoy as sharply. It is also because in Plotinus I find a faith in substance although it is not my faith, while in the moderns who think of themselves as the enlightened of Hume (I do not think they get all of Hume) I find only a frivolous or rigid determination to get along without anything more really there than the least possible, or impossible.

Yet there is a sharp falling away in Neoplatonism from the interest that kept substance central in Greek thinking from Thales to Aristotle. The social condition of the Mediterranean world deteriorated rapidly as the Greek city-states and the Greek citizens, having survived Macedon, were swamped in the Roman Empire; it improved in the first half of the second century under the four "good emperors," only to become worse with and after the son of the best of the good four, Commodus the son of Marcus. The interest after Aristotle is moral and salvatory: intellectually and nobly in the Epicureans and Stoics, more desperately beyond. In the earlier decline there were, for example, the gnostics, pre-Christian and Christian heretics, whom Hans Jonas likens to our existentialists. With them appears the view, definite in third-century Neoplatonism, that matter is at best non-good as nonbeing or is evil. Thus for the gnostics, the creator is a demon, fabricating tormented matter; and the good God, if there is one, beyond the unpleasant Demiurge is very far beyond and to be reached, or worshiped without reaching, only by sheer commitment to heroism. Thus from the death of Aristotle in 322 B.C. to Augustine, who was Bishop of Hippo in A.D. 400, or indeed to the coming of Arabic numerals and the ontological argument about A.D. 1000, there is soon increasing and generally assured other-worldiness and anti-intellectualism. These color the doctrines of conduct and of knowledge; they also mean that substance is thought of as removed, a postulate of faith not a topic of observation, encounter, imagination, and curiosity.

It is also the case that substance, the metaphysics of substance, is a dry topic for one in trouble or in a hurry. And it was further the case that the classic Greeks and Aristotle in particular had done both too well and too inconclusively. Fashions change in philosophy as in clothes. Aristotle topped many discussions of substance with the long, very difficult, apparently inconclusive *Metaphysics*. "We are not Aristotle, or Plato, or Pythagoras," said the Alexandrians. "Let us think of how to save our souls; or collect stories; or edit texts. And if we have an illumination which is clearly true we will say, 'Pythagoras himself said it; *ipse dixit*.'" Controversies not infrequently are just put aside, usually after getting hotter, degenerating in quality, getting tiresome. We see this much more with the question of substance in modern controversy; but there was some of it in the age after Aristotle.

I left a choice between A.D. 400 and 1000 because Christianity did much to bring back the view that the material world is really there, has being, and is not evil, the view that the individual soul endures and its aim is not the loss of its selfhood, the view that the creator is kindly or may be, and the view that history is real as making a difference in its preparation of the next world, not just lapsing into another one. It is true that Clement and Origen, the great theorists of the second half of the third century, when Christianity and Neoplatonism were contending, were themselves near "Platonism" and that the church took over items from its vanquished after the victory. I believe that Christianity owed no small part of its appeal for the middle and upper classes of the Mediterranean world to its re-offering of something of the more common-sense world view of the Academics and most of the classic Greeks and that it especially appealed by its use of individual continuation in the next life as built and partly earned in this. The Athenian or even Spartan of the fifth century had been a difference-making part of a difference-making city. In the third century A.D. not even the Roman citizen made any difference in the running of the Empire. The Christian said, "What you do makes no difference to Rome. But what the humblest of you does makes a difference, while God and his angels watch what is done in this world, as a part of that supernatural drama which builds the City of God, in the eternal life you move on into beyond this life." So came back the feeling of importance.

There are better arguments than the feeling of importance for the necessity of the being of substance; but there is no better subjective persuasion of the substantiality of that which feels important—indeed, if one is persuaded that something feels important, one feels that if that other feels truly then that other is substance. But although Christianity owed something of its success against Neoplatonism, against Julian, whom the Christians call the Apostate, to its offering of material and personal and historical realism, Christianity did not analyze or argue these realisms or renew Aristotle's discussions of the grammar of substance. Augustine was concerned with Man and men and the origination of sin, a special instance of the danger of taking species words as Platonic "Ideas" and then supposing that an "Idea" ever does anything at all. The same danger is made hieroglyphic for the coming Middle Ages in the nevertheless splendid gift of Boethius' translation of (the Neoplatonist) Porphyry's commentary on Aristotle, in which the "tree of Porphyry" gives Socrates, Plato, Aristotle as the three *infimae species* of the species man and where species appears as a fifth one of the "heads of predicables." During the 500 years of the Dark Ages there is only Scotus Erigena, who returned to Europe from the relative remnant-learning of North England–Ireland; and he gives us his own version of Plotinus and the pseudo-Dionysius.

The view of substance in the Middle Ages is a topic for a specialist, and I am not he. The first period, of Anselm and Abelard, attracts me more, but it will suffice to say that it seems to me that Anselm's ontological argument, whether or not it proves God, does prove substance. If anything is, then of what is there is that which is most independent, most able to get along and to do, and this is substance; and the fool is wrong to say in his heart that there is no substance. Even Whitehead's "least puff of experience," if all alone in existence, is substance—although the name would offend Whitehead, and I am unwilling to offend with a name if he will let me have the thing (that "least whiff" and even all of "experience" being less than I want as we disagree over our words and our things). The ontological argument can also offer to prove the authority of positive or convergent ideals: beyond the many crookeds there is one straight, one beauty, one good. Even in existence it may be said there must be a straightest, at least one, or more, than which there is no straighter; but this does not seem important. It is more important that the ontological argument does not even seem to offer a proof of the negatives: of a perfectly crooked, ugly, bad; of the devil. I think this does suggest the natural integralness of substance as involving both being and value, and so, inferentially, of knowing:

there is no pure "contemplative" knowing of descriptive, nonvaluational, fact; and no purely practical experiencing, or added-on volitional asserting of value. Anselm, Abelard, Bernard of Clairvaux may have had some such vision, coming before analysis had divorced the integral.

The later medieval theories seem grand in their conspectus and acute in their details but bemused by obscurities of "individual essences" and "substantial forms." Some of these, European theory has never escaped or escaped only by sacrificing substance.

CHAPTER III

CARTESIAN SIMPLES

The determining facts about Descartes and the official start of the modern theory of substance are that, like Francis Bacon, Descartes was a teacher of a method assertedly new, operating without assumptions and potent to achieve formal and natural science; that, like Bacon, he was sure the natural world is one of body in motion; that, like Bacon, he at first saw no way to prove this by his method and indeed his method seemed to depend upon it; but that, unlike Bacon, Descartes then thought he found a way by his method to establish the sort of world his method needed to create physics (and medicine). Unlike Bacon, he wanted for his method and his mathematical physics not "body" in Bacon's feeling for body but a purely geometric matter and motion. So came about the partly paradoxical story—his proof of the physical world started with the personal self, his own subject, in the *cogito ergo sum*: I think therefore I am; then his physics of geometrized matter, an abstractly simple stuff, worked back under and into the personalistic, individualistic, substantialism from which it grew; it turned that ego soul into an item of a mind stuff, a "thinking substance"; and this, which in the beginning meant a substance that thinks (with the natural plural of "substances that think"), became a thinking out of which individual thinkers are somehow composed or in which they are somehow comprised. I have severely capsuled a detailed story, one which perhaps never crystallized out completely. Here one may merely reflect that if Francis Bacon had followed a similar path he might have come out with a worse physics than Descartes' and a better view of thing and self.

Descartes is rightly known for the clarity of his writing. Yet his first book (not early, he was thirty-three), the *Rules for the Direction of the Mind*, is extremely obscure until you know what he is trying to say and does not feel he has the right to say. After the first two paragraphs in explanation of Rule XII (and right here is where selections in books of readings are apt to cut off), he says what amounts to "Let us just play as though," and then light begins to fall on the doctrine, on the Cartesian method. But the make-believe is not enough and presently the teacher walks out and the incomplete book was not published. Then came the finding of the way and its exposition in the *Discourse on Method*. But the reader may not catch the timeliness and import of the finding; he may wonder at the emphasis on method in the title of the little book which is mostly read and remembered for bits of Descartes' biography and for the *cogito ergo sum*. It is precisely the *cogito* and the derivation from it which allowed Descartes to set up the physical world his method craved and so set up the method itself. It is doubtless true that if the system could in its own right set up the world it needs for physics, that world could be set up as wider than or prior to physics. But it was only the illumination of the *cogito* that let Descartes find the data of Cartesian clarity and distinctness and simplicity, aside from and back of his mathematics (which gave him no existence) and his mathematical matter and motion (which were yet unsure). He could then move on to the nature he believed in and his method rejoiced in. The argument is given, with insistent brevity, in three of the four major publications, beginning with the *Discourse*, and in a slightly longer but easily excerptible form in an unpublished dialogue.

I noticed that whilst I thus wished to think all things false, it was absolutely essential that the "I" who thought this should be somewhat, and remarking that this truth "*I think, therefore I am*" was so certain and so assured that all the most extravagant suppositions brought forward by the sceptics were incapable of shaking it, I came to the conclusion that I could receive it without scruple as the first principle of the Philosophy for which I was seeking. [*Discourse*, Part IV]

Of a surety I myself did exist since I persuaded myself of something or merely because I thought of something. But there is some deceiver or other, very powerful and very cunning, who ever employs his ingenuity in deceiving me. Then without doubt I exist also if he deceives me, and let him deceive me as much as he will, he can never cause me to be nothing so long as I think I am something. So that after having reflected well and carefully examined all things, we must come to the definite conclusion that this proposition: I am, I exist, is necessarily true each time that I pronounce it, or that I mentally conceive it. [*Meditations*, II]

While we thus reject all that of which we can possibly doubt, and feign that it is false, it is easy to suppose that there is no God, nor heaven, nor bodies, and that we possess neither hands, nor feet, nor indeed any body; but we cannot in the same way conceive that we who doubt these things are not; for there is a contradiction in conceiving that what thinks does not, at the same time as it thinks, exist. And hence this conclusion *I think, therefore I am*, is the first and most certain of all that occurs to one who philosophises in an orderly way. [*Principles*, I, vii]

Can you doubt of your doubt and remain uncertain whether you doubt or not? . . . Since then you cannot deny that you doubt, and that it is on the other hand certain that you doubt, and so certain that you cannot even doubt of that, it is likewise true that you are, you who doubt; and that is so true that you can no longer doubt of it any more.—I agree with you, for if I did not exist I could not doubt. [*The Search after Truth*.]

The argument, as controversy since has shown, needs two allowances. Descartes does not note them, but he would have no objection to noting them, except waste of time, for he takes both to be altogether clear and allowed by anyone. First: when one "thinks," it is sometimes quite sure, to him, that he does so; consciousness is its own guarantee, and for itself in the end there is no need for, and there cannot be, any other. Second: when there is thinking, there is a thinker; when there is any doing, there is something that does. There is also a stipulation to be kept in understanding the argument as given: Descartes is using "think" in the widest possible sense: "think," "*penser*," "*cogitare*"— each is the genus for all the species of consciously sensing, remembering, hoping, fearing, wondering, doubting, believing, denying, calculating, loving, hating, hurting, enjoying. But this is verbal and is expressly stipulated by Descartes several times. Its neglect leads some to call the argument "overintellectual." With these provisos, it may be that the argument is best put in the negative. It cannot be both that-I-do-not-exist and that-I-think; that is to say, if I do not exist, I do not think. But I do think. Therefore I exist. This is *tollendo tollens*: by denying the consequent I deny the antecedent; and it has the same accepted validity as the affirmative *ponendo ponens,* both in older logic and in the symbolic calculus of propositions. An advantage of the *tollendo* is that the *ponendo* is sometimes read: "If I drink cyanide I die, I drink cyanide, therefore I am dead." So: "If I think, I am; I think, therefore I am"; and the thinking is taken as the cause of the being. But Decartes' argument is, as the medievals would say, in "*ratione cognoscendi*" not "*essendi.*" Existing is the necessary, indispensable condition for thinking: thinking does not cause existence, existence allows thinking and without existence there is no thinking. So when we know there is existent thinking we know there is an existent thinker. Do we ever directly know there is thinking apart from our existing? No, only each may know that he thinks: there is his thinking, he thinks, he is. We cannot simply convert the hypothetical; we may not deny the antecedent or affirm the consequent. Descartes never doubted there is existence without thinking.

The late Crane Brinton said that Descartes was such a fine gentleman and philosopher that he did not consider "I sweat, therefore I am." [1] I do not know that Descartes ever considered sweating as a function of substance, but walking comes in for notice more than once (as with Hobbes) in the *Objections and Replies* published with the *Meditations*. Unquestionably the proposition "If I walk I am" is as true a hypothetical as "If I think I am"; but how is one to know he walks? How can he get the sure categorical to add as a minor premise to his hypothetical major premise? Only the unique reflexivity, or perhaps better the self-presentation, of consciousness can give it. All that walks, or sweats, or does anything, or changes in itself, is; but only those things that think can prove to themselves that they are. I sometimes now feel that at least every organic doing has its ingredient of consciousness, of awareness; if this be so, then neither walking nor sweating need be altogether removed from the potentiality of the *cogito*. But Descartes does not need to say this nor do I need to grant these "*petites perceptions*" the ability to see implications, even the most direct. It is only sufficiently "high" awareness that can add to its self-assuredness of object the embroidery of the subject "Therefore I am." Descartes did not think that rocks or the soulless animals can prove their existence, for all that they exist. And I suspect he would say the dreamer, although vividly aware, must awake before he can truthfully assert that he can prove to himself that he exists. (This might do some hurt to Descartes' use of dreaming, but that to-do about dreaming has seemed to me to do some hurt to his teaching and more to those who came after him.)

1. *Ideas and Men* (New York, 1950), p. 350.

The belief that thinking needs a thinker has been more the focus of attack, as by Bertrand Russell—all we have, it is said, is: if I think, then there is thinking—and it is here that the subject-predicate sentence and Aristotelian grammar are regularly brought out to explain the error of all of us who believe in things. I rather like grammar, Aristotelian and otherwise, but I do not think it is addiction to grammar that makes it hard to understand doing without a doer; it just is hard to understand. I shall not say it is another grammar, or a lack of grammar, that leads to a theory of absolute modalities, nor shall I invite the habitué of those difficult realms to the ease of a language which permits itself substantives. But someone who insists on a dance without a dancer, on two dances-together without dancers with one another, on dances-together co-ordinated with music that has no players, and on a dance-together that enrages the jealousy of a non-dance without a non-dancer—such a one I suspect of belonging to that stern modernism which requires a philosopher to eschew anything understandable if sufficient ingenuity can rig up a substitute remotely intelligible. Also I more than suspect of myself that a radical bias, an ease and an unease, makes me less than fair here (although I am sure I am right).

Although I am willing to accept the validity of the argument and the truth of the conclusion of the *cogito*, I want to step aside from Descartes' next and rapid step. Since, he says, it is by my thinking that I prove I exist, it must be that my whole essence is to think, that I am a "thinking thing," and that I must always think and can do nothing else except accidentally. Each of these seems a simple *non sequitur*. If mice were the only squeakers, we could know their presence by squeaking; they would not have to squeak all the time and not eat. By the nature of the argument, being aware is the only way for us to be sure of the proof of our existence. I happen to think that being aware, "thinking," is most important; but the argument is not that important: few are concerned about it and no one spends all his time getting set for it. It might be said that all we have proved at first is that there is a thinking thing; but we have done nothing to prove that the thinking thing is always thinking or that the thinking thing is not also a thing of many other sorts. It may be that Descartes is already looking ahead to matter, knows that this thinking thing he has got is just the soul and not the whole self, wants a matter of a single "attribute," is thus pleased with a soul symmetrically with a single attribute, and, having proved the existence of the self on a substantial assumption, now within a paragraph settles for a mind and a body which are at best quasi-substantial, aspects of the self, following the rule of simple characters and not the rule of actual things.

It is not yet, however, that the full flat symmetrical picture is made clear by Descartes, or probably is clear to him. He still usually if not always in the *Discourse* speaks of a soul or souls, a mind or minds (the idiom for things); not of soul or mind (the idiom for aspect or stuff). He is already speaking of body not of a body, the body, or bodies. (There is one translation of the key paragraph in the *Discourse* about the nature of "myself" which uses "the body" and "bodies" along with "the mind," but a comparison of the French and Latin shows the symmetry is not yet established.)[2] The theory of matter is not expounded until the last of the *Meditations*. And the full symmetry is not reached, and not always kept then, until the *Principles*, where we are given the (unfortunate) definition of substance, told that a substance as such has one and only one attribute,

---

2. One nice thing about Cartesian study is that we have both the French and the Latin versions, which if not both by Descartes at least had his approval.

and informed that there are two "created substances," mind and matter, with the attributes of thinking and extension. Thus the individual self that the *cogito* in the beginning proved to exist, it now seems must have been cut like a biscuit out of the dough of "mind substance."

Let us go back now and follow the celebrated steps of the argument: I prove my existence; then in three ways I prove the existence of God—by Anselm's ontological argument (since the notion of God necessarily involves his existence), by the argument from cause (since I now know there is some existence, myself, that I cannot have brought into being), and by what Descartes thought of as most his own reasoning, from my idea of "objective" perfection which like any idea must have a source of as much "formal" reality as the idea has objectively.[3] The God I have proved is a veracious God, so that now I can take the evidence of my senses—not uncritically, since a philosopher must provide for error as well as for knowledge. That repeated and massive evidence, checked by my intellect, assures me the world is real; and, since what I cannot think away from matter is extension, Descartes is assured that the attribute of matter is extension, that all matter is extended and whatever is extended is matter. This doctrine of matter makes somewhat the same difficulties on the physical side as the doctrine that dreamless sleep is impossible makes on the psychological side; but the difficulty of the division and aggregation of material things is much less acute than the, to me impossible, one of separating and associating minds, souls, or selves. Motion seems to be taken as involved in extension, so we

3. Descartes and his contemporaries, it will be recalled, continued the Scholastic use of "objective" and "formal." Cf. this from his *Reply to Objections I:* ". . . the idea of the sun will be the sun itself existing in the mind, not indeed formally, as it exists in the sky, but objectively, i.e., in the way in which objects are wont to exist in the mind. . . ."

have a Democritean (but not atomic) world of size, shape, position, and motion—with the splendid addition of Cartesian geometry. The usage of Kepler and Galileo, the basically similar faith of Bacon, the basis of modern physics is now legitimized. We are so accustomed to it and to its success that we have to stop to feel the courage needed to assume it, the call for some sort of justification. Why should a thin realm of qualityless moving shapes, working in seemingly full independence and authority, eventuate exactly and intricately in the multifariously qualitative world we find in our acquaintance? Surely its success has been such that we would be niggardly to mute our applause of its formulator. His own immediate use is now apt to be forgotten. One of his translators and editors, not always a eulogist, says of the three essays published with the *Discourse* (the *Meteors*, the *Dioptric*, the *Geometry*) that never elsewhere has so much original truth been given the world at one time.

It is a curious fact of history that never, I think, has one admittedly great man been made the target for so much objection from all sorts of angles as has Descartes in the last couple of generations. For one example: no one ever went so far, and so early, to announce the computer ideal. His animal was pure automaton; his man as nearly such as he could make him—and nearer than is often noticed. He might well be first in the electronic-brain hagiography if it allowed itself one. Instead, Descartes seems the one philosopher computer people know to set up and shoot at. And here I am, a Cartesian in many ways, shooting at him because I think he diverted the doctrine of substance.

His definition of substance in *Principles*, I, li, is "that which needs no other thing in order to exist." This, I find written in the margin of my first text of the *Principles*, "gives it to Spinoza."

Indeed Descartes recognizes this in the next sentence

and says that by this definition only God can be substance. But, "having" God and being in a hurry to get on to what he is excited about, physics, he contents himself with adding that his mind and matter need only God and each other and so they can quite well be called "created substances." He does not stop to notice that his abstract characterization of mind and matter, extreme in one direction, and his definition of "substance," extreme in the other direction, not only give his case to Spinoza but give it to Hume and Bertrand Russell in the future argumentation, to bottomless phenomenalism beyond unindividuated substantialism. The trouble is not that his mind and matter are not altogether up to the job of absolute independence: they are not up to substantial existence at all. God may keep us in constant illusion of mental and material aspects; but once mind and matter have been restricted to a single essence, one attribute, they cannot exist except as adjectival, truth or illusion, the aspects of something or nothing. If mind has no nature but thinking, there can be no firm resistance to saying that "I think therefore I am" may prove that there is thinking but not any I. If matter has no nature but extension, there can be no firm resistance to saying that on Descartes' argument the veracity of God justifies our belief in the dependability of the laws of physics but not in physical bodies. This is obscured for us by our feeling for the bodily existence of "matter," but the logic of the difference is illustrated by the Continental refusal to include hardness, impenetrability, among the "primary qualities" where the English liked to have it.

That substance requires existential independence we have already said and used as a mark of substance, but it does not require (or in my view allow) total independence of other actual existences. An adjective, a character, a mode must "wait for"—needs—the existence of a thing to allow its adjectival existence. But a substance, existing "for itself," does exist, and to exist is to do and suffer, to be correlated and contingent in its community of existences. Substance is distinguished by its contingence from the eternal characters, and by its independence it is distinguished from the characters in their appearing. "This man or this horse" is independent, but not of the earth he stands on, the food he eats, or the parents that brought him into the world. (I know that this may be put down as the metaphysical working out of my grammatical acceptance.)

The knowledge side of the Cartesian crux deserves attention. It is a commonplace that Descartes is a visualist, even more than most of us. It is the field of the seen to which he turns and it seems not only that it is that field which he helped make basic for modern physics and science generally but also that it is that field which is naturally best for a mathematical physics. The Cartesian purification of body to matter and of matter to extension goes along. If Francis Bacon had traveled Descartes' path (and he profoundly wanted such a path), he might well have repeated the *cogito* in his own magnificent, humanist, legal language; he might likewise have stopped to prove the existence of God, probably in a more Puritanic fashion; but the world which the veracity of God would have guaranteed to his humanist, legal, and dramatic way of knowing would surely have been one of body in motion. But the motion would have been qualitative (in his lists of "simple motions" he does not even include mere change of co-ordinates, which for Descartes is all there is), and body would have been body, not matter, would have been closer to biology, certainly not bare extension. Some of this theme will reappear with quantum physics, and with some recent biology and psychology.

Visualism is even more important, I take it, in the birth and growth of phenomenalist antisubstantialism, but it is less appropriate than in physics. Without the (perhaps false but natural) supposition of picture-like visual images it is hard to believe we could have made up the notion of "knowledge" as a spread-out and continuing content, which then ate up both of its Cartesian progenitors, the known world and the knowing mind. The doctrinal child has outlived its encouraging circumstances, for it still seems to be very wide and very deep (if so one-surface a theory can be deep). Yet there have been, for long now, some welcome recognitions of our richer awareness—a spreading of notice not only from sight to the other external senses of Aristotle and to some of the "internal" sensations like pain, heat, motion, and effort, but to others, for many of which we have no name and indeed no imaginative location. How do you know we are hungry? became my favorite annoying question for a while.

One side effect of this development and shift, an effect already seen in post-Cartesian theory, is more important in twentieth-century theory and will later receive more attention. The other senses by comparison with sight, the sensations by comparison with the senses, the less familiarly named or placed awarenesses by comparison with such as pleasure and pain, are all—without argument and in part properly—put on a graduated scale of increasing subjectivity. So the rescue of one of the great needs of modern philosophy, the need for a more hospitable doctrine of awareness, is apt to make war on the effort to answer another great need of modern philosophy, the need for more realism. The intracutaneous is surely more subjective as more my own, less "common" (in Heraclitus's precious phrase), but it is not more subjective as more "mental," more just "a puff of experience," less real or substantial in its occurrence.

Vision I believe to be realistic and direct; I do not see any "ideas" or images or representations. For all that, it is distant; what I see is out there, perhaps far out there, and always at least a little back there in time; it may be dangerous to say so, but vision occurs by message. By contrast, my stomach ache is the actual talk of my actual stomach here and now. Representationists ("dualists") have trouble knowing what to do with sensations that do not represent anything and yet on their theory have to be mental; and presentationists ("monists") have trouble explaining how sensations differ from perceptions. And beyond, we have more needs and more difficulties. Is "a feeling of sadness and longing that is not akin to pain" more subjective than the stomach ache and in which sense? And what of those external but not clearly sensual awarenesses which may be the most dramatically needful of any? How do we know good? How do we know each other? If you believe the story of "sense data" and "argument by analogy," very well; I do not.

This is not just a business of welcoming new, or un-named, or unspecified modes of awareness as though they were additional senses or sensations or feelings—a process which has its appeal but which is properly suspect by any economical psychologist as well as by the positivist. Of spe-cial importance is the information we get in the imposed and gradually controlled commotion of our motions and the motions and resistances of the other things in the midst of which we live. Like Descartes, I am a man of the eye; and as a student I went along the way on which the eye took modern philosophy. But I was a child before I was a stu-dent. It may be I remember my childhood more than most do. But Aristotle tells us that touch, at least the response to pressure, is the most widely distributed of the senses, and psychology tells us the child has months of this before it can use its eyes. And in remembered childhood every child knows touch and the pressures of the world upon him and many lessons of this sort of living before he can do much of anything about following the curiosity of the eye, even though the glory and wonder of seeing may already be there.

In the course of studentship I came to cast back into my "Prelude" to seek kinetic refuge from the "problem of induction" and from phenomenalism—refuge in what I call the "rolling-down-the-hill doctrine." Even before rolling a child has learned not to fall, learned to crawl, to walk; and in these learnings-to has learned many thats—the principles of the natural world. Long before geometry and physics and anatomy, and with more assurance than observation and study will ever give, the child knows the different ways in which a round body and a flat body go down a hill and he feels the needfulness of the difference. We do not "induce" principles from observations counted up and calculated by probability. We need repetition of doing, some, but this is because our muscular understanding is, like our rational, stupid in one way or another. We "see the universal in the particular," Aristotle says of his "intuitive induction," and so our interacting bodies feel it.

We begin to get the principles which will later puzzle our theories in our earlier pre-theoretic doings. So we begin the faith in our bodily substantiality before there is any verbal problem. I have said that I suppose it is only substance in some relatively absolute and absolutely relative sense that can be proved by some sort of ontological argument. But my own going on as an enduring, active, and suffering participator among bodily things fortifies my faith in substance as what is really there in a bodily way and as what gives basis to the memory and choice and effort that I knew earlier and know now more surely than I know any phenomenon or phenomena.

John Locke's football between the hands and Dr. Johnson's retort to Bishop Berkeley may bring us back to this. The world of mental content which philosophy is about to fall into soon after Descartes, and which Cartesian dualism and visualism probably led into, is not itself Descartes'. His thinking substance was soul-stuff, thinking, not what was thought about. Just what Descartes meant by "idea" is unclear, looking back through the mist of Locke and later philosophers. And when I plead for an acquaintance richer than his visualism of extension plus the secondary qualities and the "passions" and richer than the later "sense data" theories, I do not want merely to add to the variety of the contents of the "mental" realm, what has since come to be called "experience." The kinetic doings and learnings especially should not be translated into mental echoes of the muscular doings and added to the subjective pictures that may or may not represent something beyond themselves or the mind. I would rather retain the real self and deny all mental content. I also find here the basic and recurrent threat of uncritical acceptance of analysis. Even while the phenomenalist reduces everything to "impressions," he distinguishes action, description, passion, value. He may say that I, in my theory, have to do the same thing externally as he does internally, and to a degree he is right. But I can leave my distinctions in my theory, in the world of abstraction, and say that substantially, in existence, these—action, description, feeling, value—never are without some element of each. It is not merely that any knowing of mine is my action: what I know, so far as it is a knowing of the existent world, is in part action. And whenever I act my action is also a knowing, a knowing of descriptive fact but also of value, a feeling on my part, and a choice. Just as Descartes' mathematical physics, visualism, analytic acumen, and simplistic method led to a physical world of pure extension, so in knowledge it allowed for the view that knowledge is basically geometrical perception and intellect, upon which is overlaid the perception of qualities, then the passions, then the will.

Spinoza accepted Descartes' definition of substance and, having accepted it, went ahead with a sort of Parmenidean straightness to mean what he said. He accepted God as substance, as the only substance, the necessary substance, and necessarily the only substance. He also accepted the adjectival nature of mind and matter (the "attributes" of God), which I find implied in Descartes' developing treatment despite his own insistence that mind and matter remained always substances. Spinoza thus gave up the individuality of substances—except the perhaps equivocal individuality of God —and the substantiality of individuals ("modes" of the attributes). Along with this are lost the individuals' interaction and intercontingence and, as Spinoza worked it out, all their freedom. In substance itself only existence remains substantial, or existence and independence. But the independence of a being that is necessarily the only being seems empty, whereas the existence is so absolute it is hard to know what existence means—it may be possible to feel but is probably impossible to say. The marks of existence, the existent's doing and being done to, have lapsed or are unreal. Time, allowed to remain as appearance for the finite mind and to remain as an understood illusion "under the aspect of eternity" for the total mind of God, is not really real, is "all there" like the "it was not nor will it be but it is" of Parmenides or the "I am that I am" of the Old Testament. So substance is an existent eternal over against and only worshipfully distinguishable from the nonexistent eternal of the numbers. This is to rescind the gift of personal importance and significance with which Christianity won the hellenistic world from neoplatonism. Spinozism is indeed a new Plotinianism, but curiously materialistic, naturalistic, antiromantic, and without emanation. It is doubtless also the case that this derivation from the words of Descartes fitted in genetically with Spinoza's study of medieval Jewish philosophy, eccentric for seventeenth-century Christian philosophers (except Ralph Cudworth).

Spinoza also took up Descartes' suggestion (*Reply* to second set of *Objections*) that he could have written the *Meditations* in "synthetic" style rather than as he did in "analytic" style (words scarcely explained, which have done damage to Cartesian study and other study since). This pickup by Spinoza from Descartes gives us the *more geometrico demonstrata* of the *Ethics*; a method which for all its logicality seems to have been logically difficult but rhetorically immensely successful for those readers who stay the course. Spinoza had already tried to write his philosophy beginning with the moral doctrine, in the *Improvement of the Understanding*, but he became slowed in the theory of knowledge and broke off the undertaking. I feel that for Spinoza the moral doctrine was always both basis and aim; but this may be merely that it is what I like: the fourth and fifth books of the *Ethics*, making serene and severe and lovely the somewhat evangelistic first pages of the *Improvement*. The cynical but sagacious psychology of the third book of the *Ethics* and its continuation in the fourth, "Of Human Bondage," I admire and, with caveats and additions, can go along with. The theology of the first book I admire and deny. The theory of knowledge of the second book I have never been able to feel I understand. But here in the *Ethics*, with the geometric method and Descartes' general program of building up from and with scientific simples, Spinoza begins with the definition of substance, the doctrine of God, and of knowledge. The moral doctrine, the doctrine of salvation, is now the achievement. Whether or not the abstract austerity of the theology and epistemology and the materialism and cynicism of the psychology are the needful premises of

the moral achievement, or whether they are sufficient premises, they are a massive substructure from which the pilgrim
emerges to conviction. Something of this massiveness derives
from what is now made first and basic, an asserted necessary
faith in a necessary substance that is both material and
spiritual, and indeed "infinitely infinite" beyond those two
known attributes.

Since knowing is what mind does, and since mind or
minds, in both Descartes and common sense, mark as individuals at least those of us things that know, the theory of
knowledge might be expected to afford a bridge from Spinoza's one substance to apparent manyness. But Spinoza
just seems to make worse (perhaps because more consistently
and economically) the Cartesian amalgamation of minds in
mind. Descartes is drawn into this only as he moves from
"I am" to "thinking substance" as the substance of all I's.
Spinoza starts with it as the thinking attribute of the one
substance, God. His theory of knowing and its relation to
the world supposedly known is expressly founded on Descartes' dualism of mind and body, without any paltering with
the story of the pineal gland or of interaction. If the person
is merely a mode, the pineal gland is a mere mode of a mode,
and attributes neither can nor need to interact. Interaction
is replaced by a parallelism of the two (for us) attributes of
God. But I am never clear which is the mental parallel: the
thinking minds or the thought contents; and, only less difficult, which is the material parallel: the material thing out
there, as when we see a star, or the physiological process, my
eye and optic nerve and brain. In any case the thing known,
if a material thing, is known only as being "in knowledge,"
and there can be no transitive meeting and no test as between
truth and error except for a test within knowledge, as in
the later "coherence theory" of truth. This is part of the

denial of common-sense substances and their dealings with one another. Aspects, attributes, even if aspects of existence, as aspects cannot know or have effects upon one another.

I suppose the rejoinder is that this is asserted by me only because I am already the sort of substantialist I am. I do not think the rejoinder is competent but it is a rejoinder one must always be aware of, and respectful of. And here it is competent to the extent of reminding me that the brevity of my disposal is unfair to the subtlety, and difficulty, of Spinoza's theory. He is little concerned about "knowing" a material thing even when that includes knowing its external relations with other things—that is, the sort of "knowledge situation" imagined most easily by believers in a correspondence theory ("the cat is on the table") does not much interest him. This is not to say that Spinoza scorns "natural" knowledge, for there is no more severely naturalistic a philosopher. But such mapping is not even the lowest of Spinoza's three stages of knowledge—hearsay, discursive, intuitive—for which he uses the illustration of the different ways of understanding the rule of three. To know for Spinoza is to know by "causes," and cause is rational, essential, not as with Hume external and "accidental."

"The order and connection of ideas is the same as the order and connection of things," he says (*Ethics*, II, vii), and we in this later age think of proper images properly arranged on a time-space chart as are the physical things in actual time and space. Thus we impose our English eighteenth-century notions of "idea" and "knowledge." (That theorem in the *Ethics* also seems, wrongly, to settle the issue of what constitutes the thinking attribute in favor of the mental-content view as against the mental-activity view.) We have to turn back to the definitions for Book II: "By idea I mean the mental conception which is formed by the mind as a thinking thing." The mind as a thinking thing forms the ideas, it is not formed by them, or composed of them. Further, "conception" is used rather than "perception" in order to "express an activity of mind." Not only is the mind, as a mode of the attribute, activity, but also the idea itself, at least as a modification of the mode, is no mere content or percept or presentation or phenomenon, but involves activity. So in a note to Book II, xlviii, he says: "For by ideas I do not mean images such as are made up behind the eye or somewhere in the brain but conceptions of thought." "Ideas" are not just material or data for thinking—they are thinking; and yet the thinking thing, the mind, is more than an assemblage of the separable and partial and partially active ideas (I believe). An enriched repetition is in a note to the next theorem at the end of the book (II, xlix), where, after an unusually diffuse buildup, he admonishes the reader to distinguish between the idea and "the images of things we imagine" and between ideas and words. We are in danger of thinking of ideas as if they were mute pictures on a tablet, and we fail to realize that an idea, just as an idea, makes an affirmation or a negation: "*non vident ideam quatenus idea est affirmationem aut negationem involvere.*" Ideas, "*veluti picturas in tabula mutas,*" are the sense data we read back, from our argumentation and from Hume and Locke, into Spinoza and Descartes; but Spinoza as it were ahead of time warns us not to.

In this note distinguishing the idea from an image, and in the emphasis upon the activity of mind and at least the logical activity (affirmation or negation) of the idea, there is help for our partial understanding of what the Continental seventeenth century meant by mind and by idea; and there is also a suggestion, unheeded so far as I know on the Continent, of an integralness in knowing and in the object of knowing which is repeated more richly by George Berkeley in eighteenth-century Britain, where it was more needed and, so far as I know, was simply unnoted. This is that "super-pragmatism" referred to earlier. The mind does not first accept or start by being composed of a loose set of simple descriptive data, then develop them with relations and "conceptual" identification, then add passion from the subjective and stew up some emotion, whereupon a still more subjective aroma of value is wafted. The mind does these all at once because they are all at once and are interfused in what the mind is aware of and is thinking about. Pragmatism tries to start with sensations of fact and find the truth or falsity of its beliefs about them by future working and choice. But choice is rather in the past, in the topic of knowledge, in the nature and natures of things. Choice is present in all natural truth, as quantity is in arithmetic; but only sentences about the future are made true or false in the future; others are true or false now regardless of our knowing or believing; and sentences about the future, as Aristotle said of "There will be a seafight tomorrow" and "There will not be a seafight tomorrow," are neither true nor false now unless they be formally so, as it is true "There will be a seafight tomorrow or there will not." Here we will find disagreement from Spinoza, for whom the future, although unknown to us, is eternally true, as well as from those who think the future, when it comes, will give a sort of *ex post facto* truth to anticipatory sentences.

Leibniz draws a quick bravo from the Aristotelian sub-stantialist, for Leibniz holds on to the belief in substance while going back to substances and individualism, which Descartes began with and never intentionally altogether gave up. Reality is monads, which are many, individual, internally spiritual and externally physical, or energy as thinking and energy as calculable extension: replacing the two created substances of Descartes, the two attributes of the one substance of Spinoza. But several themes in this most ingenious of theoreticians tend to mute the bravo. Retaining most of the definition of substance as given by Descartes, Leibniz safeguards the independence of his monads by cutting off all interaction of monads. So disappears the doing and being done to. The monads were, to be sure, created, "fulgurated," by God and are maintained by God, but they have no dealings with their fellow monads. Leibniz keeps change but it must be change inside each monad. Also, since time and space are not monads they are not really there except in the perception of the monad. So on two grounds "the monad has no windows": the monad must not compromise its independence, and what use is a window if there is no space beyond it through which to see? Leibniz nevertheless has no thought of giving up the cosmos character of the world; no world is more thoroughly systematized than his. So while I have no windows, I seem to see, and what I see must go along with what you see. Spinozistic parallelism will do within the monad, but as between different monads there is a nonparallel harmonization. So we are introduced to the Great Principle of the Pre-established Harmony, of which Leibniz is most proud but which common sense has always found most unacceptable. Each monad has the course of its seeing, of all its "thinking," laid down from the beginning, and laid down differently from but in precise harmony with the courses of all the other monads. This incidentally requires an exactitude of determinism from which any lover of liberty will shy, probably even more than from the eternalistic determinism of Spinoza, because now he has felt himself in a world that promised some more-than-illusory activity.

Associated with this pre-established harmony, but probably with some difference in origin, is another Great Principle—the Identity of Indiscernibles: if two things can show no characteristic difference, they are not two but one. This precludes duplication in the system of nature, the world of monads, while the Principle of Sufficient Reason—interpreted under the Platonic, Western, optimism that it is better to be than not to be and that the creator is a creator of plenitude—precludes gaps. The origin and motive of these provisions may lie in the fact that Leibniz, like Descartes, is a great mathematician and tends to find rescue and resource in mathematics. The line must have no gaps and no duplicated points. More generally: it is undenied that if any two characters—numbers, forms, shapes, qualities, abstractions— can show no difference, they are not two but one; for their being is in their character. But this appals the substantialist. For him his existence is radical to his characters; if he were to meet some fellow exactly like himself, he would still say "You are you and I am I." The principle of the identity of indiscernibles is apt to convince the reader that, in the upshot, existence for Leibniz is only mathematical existence; that reality and the meaning of substance are being retracted, as in some interpretations of Platonism, into the eternal "Ideas," with the world of sense and action demoted to a realm of "shadows and reflections in the water."

Yet Leibniz surely meant to be true to substance. The word and the notion were still revered by the three great Continentals when substantialism, as a result of its overreverend definition by some Scholastics and the Continentals, was beginning to be uncomfortable in England. Perhaps in the doctrine of "the ideality of time and space," a doctrine likely to be uncongenial to the realist and so to the substantialist, a way may be found—at least the superingenuity of Leibniz could have found a way—to mitigate the evident abstracting and formalizing effect of the principle of the identity of indiscernibles. Time and space are troublesome for the Aristotelian substantialist. He can hardly declare them individual substances: what is he to do with them in a world he has said is made up of individual substances? He does not want to try to think of them as "subjective" or just "in mental content," especially if he does not believe in such quasi-existences; and anyway if they are just seeming, they infect (if they do not disallow) the plurality and the doing and being done to of the substantial individuals already begun with. Leibniz is willing (I think lamentably) to give up the interaction of the monads and to make up for it with pre-established harmony. Does he mean then to put time and place just "in the idea," in "experience," in "the phenomenal way we see things"? This again may be to read some of Locke, Hume, and Kant back into their more innocent predecessors. The difference of time-space "points of view" of the different monads, especially if taken with a certain degree of realism, should at least allow for the truth of the principle of the identity of indiscernibles without relegating the monads to the limbo of the necessary and the nonexistent. Perhaps all he must deny of time and space is that they are antecedently real, emptinesses into which things and events may be put and which would be unaffected if all things and events were to be taken out.

Time and space may be, as some have rather superiorly liked to say, "nothing but the relations of things and events"; but if the things and events are really there and so are their relations, then neither time-space nor thing-event is mental, or more mental than the other, or "ideal" in any subjectivistic sense. Both are together and are not to be met separately in experience. But time-space and time and space can be thought of separately, as in geometry. Earlier I have embraced the position that predicates (which when simple are the "Platonic Ideas") exist only in the substantial things, which cannot exist without them; but that predicates are ideal in the sense that they can be thought of separately, and as such are abstract, and unsubstantial, and real and eternal. I try now to think of time and space as universal or collective predicates, which do not appear and disappear in the changing natures of substances but in which and by means of which the substances change. Time and space are not substances but, since substances "really" are in external relations among each other, time and space are as substantial as the shapes and durations and causations of the things. But they are not emptinesses, antecedent or logically prior. Plato's "receptacle" might possibly be, but has not been, interpreted favorably to such an existential ideality, such a relational realism of time and space as I am suggesting.

So far as I know, Leibniz. nowhere says this. But he wanted to be a substantialist, and this time-space doctrine might have let him keep substance and also keep his insistence (partly for moral reasons) on developing his monadology on the model of a mathematical continuum. At any rate, the path suggested is the way I go to work time and space substantially in.

It is still easily the case that I am no monadologist. The determinism appals me; and I do not like the movement to atomism and point analysis. I would rather struggle with the dissolving individuality of a cloud than struggle to get my own individuality out of the clustering multitude of my cells—even with the unexplained help of a chief monad. Furthermore, the parallelism, the abstention from all interaction, makes, even more than it did in Spinoza, for the growth of a myth of a flow of mental content which is soon to swallow up the self with which it began. I doubt if Leibniz had succumbed to the myth or would have welcomed the standard instructorial device of the movie that goes on, from the moment of fulguration, inside the monad and makes up all the monad's knowing. Yet this sort of "idealism" is almost required if not consciously accepted in the double-aspect theory of Leibniz, and is generally indicated for a development of the substantial but analytical dualism of Descartes. The same subjectivism, the "way of the idea," pushed to the surface even before Leibniz in the more empirical and psychological fashion of Thomas Hobbes.

CHAPTER IV

THE ENGLISH WAY OF IDEAS

Hobbes, born eight years before Descartes, was slow to publish in philosophy but outlived both Descartes and Spinoza. It is his contribution to the *Objections and Replies* that go with Descartes' *Meditations* that the reader is apt to turn to with most interest—and be disappointed. The two great thinkers and writers read as though each had set himself not to understand the other. But if at first one learns chiefly that the little Frenchman and the big Englishman did not easily take to one another, there are lights beyond, upon each; and Hobbes makes emphatic what is a general characteristic of this first set of criticisms of Descartes—what it is that sets it off from our criticisms. There is very little dissent from the *cogito*, although it may be that the ready disposition to accept the conclusion held off any acerbity of criticism of the argument as an argument. But there is frequent echo of Hobbes's contention that there is no reason to restrict the conclusion to a disembodied mind and there is obvious reason to suppose that any existence proved will be of a body, whether or not it be also a mind. Men of the mid-twentieth century, reading these objections of the mid-seventeenth, if they note the difference, will, I suppose, just excuse those predecessors as not having been let in on the fallacious leading of the subject-predicate sentence and Aristotelian grammar. But I have heard all that, many times, (but have also read and compared Aristotle and Whorf and Korzybski) and find myself closer to Hobbes and even Gassendi than to Russell or Husserl.

Hobbes seems to me to be a Baconian (he had been

one of Bacon's secretaries and helpers in the days of the
Latinizing of the *De augmentis scientiarum* from the *Advancement of Learning*), although he was not clearly aware
of this; and back of his disagreement with Descartes as to
the logic of the *cogito* is the fact that for him the sole components of the world are bodies and their basic motion is endeavor, whereas for Descartes the components are geometrical matter and basic motion is difference of co-ordinates. For
Hobbes the world is bodies in motion. The most apparent
strangeness is appearance itself; for some of these bodies
"have within themselves the patterns" of other things: they
are bodies that have acquaintance with other bodies, often
at considerable distance. Motions coming from the things
out there, through the bodily medium, into the physiological
body with its sense organs, up to the central brain, are there
met by a push back (origin of the "ejection theory") which
makes the thing out where it is rather than in where the
pushing back of the motion is. In some sense, then and there,
where the internal motion is, is the "phantasm," not the
thing but the caused appearance of the thing to me. Hobbes's
story of the sensing process, repeated in several books, has an
imaginable clarity that makes it the platform for later physical and psychological theories. The word "phantasm," and
its meaning, as well as its reference—which seems to be
definitely to a subjective, picture-like, "mental content,"
although this reference is denied in the statement that the
phantasm "too is nothing but motion"—all this is the most
effectuating of the line of tentative and partial internalizations and picturizations of our ways of knowing. This line
comes down from the "form without matter" of Aristotle,
through the "intentional species" of the Scholastics, and the
"perceptions of the senses" and ambiguous "ideas" of Descartes, Spinoza, and Leibniz. Hobbes felt the danger of the
word and soon avoided it. (He had used "apparition" in the

earlier *Human Nature,* and given it up.) And the sturdy materialist, or better corporealist, never toyed with any weakening of his assurance that there is only body in motion (which therefore the phantasm must be) and never thought of doubting that even the most distorted of waking phantasms is an effect and communication of the thing outside. But calling it a "pattern in" the perceiving body (probably an echo from the "form" of Aristotle's *De anima*) gets it into the perceiver and out of the outside; giving it the dream or ghost name of "phantasm" makes it an image not only in the body but "in the mind." When he then adds, as he does several times, that "all knowledge is from the phantasm," he sets a clear path for John Locke, agnosticism, idealism, and phenomenalism.

I think he should bravely (and despite his acknowledgment of timidity Hobbes never lacked at least dialectical bravery) have held on to his corporealism and asserted that some bodies have the trick of being aware of other bodies, and of their own bodies. Surely if there is one indicated starting element, one acquaintance in terms of which other acquaintances are to be explained, one epistemological indefinable, it should be knowing itself—knowing in the radical and widest sense as including all varieties of aware response or initiation and in the narrowest sense as abstracting from all the varying accompaniments knowing has in the varieties. "Of all appearings the most extraordinary, and ordinary, is appearing itself," to paraphrase Hobbes just verbally. If it be a phantasm or an idea we know, or a toothache or a star, or a story of history or a theorem of mathematics, the perfectly familiar and perfectly inexplicable fact of knowing is there as is the fact known. The interposition of a phantasm, an idea, still leaves the same grasp by me of the phantasm and meanwhile creates a new and perhaps hopeless problem of why what is "in my mind" somehow looks like what I am supposed to be knowing. This does not prove there are no phantasms or ideas. There may be; there may be nothing else, I suppose, in pure intelligibility, although that to me is indeed phantasmal. And no student of Lovejoy would ever deny that the representational theory, the phantasm, does do something to ease the problem of error. But to make true knowing preposterous is a heavy price to pay for the sake of making false seeming a little more easily imaginable as a histrionic deception or miscarriage.

Hobbes, with his Baconian-Milesian doctrine of integral body, could have made this acceptance and assertion as it could not be made in the abstract materialism of Descartes' world or in the corpuscular but still devitalized mechanism of the Boyle-Newton physics. But the phantasm got in the way. (And it is possible I am wrong about, and probable that he did not clearly realize, his difference from the more fashionable and more abstract sort of materialism.) A Milesian-Baconian-Aristotelian doctrine of substance could have led to a more hospitable doctrine of perception and so diverted, or pointed out an alternative to, the coming phenomenalism. And a more hospitable doctrine of perception could have diverted, or pointed out an alternative to, the slipping away of substance into the abstracted stuff against which our postphenomenalist philosophers have rebelled. Something was attempted by Hobbes's contemporaries the Cambridge Platonists, especially Henry More, and then by Anthony Ashley Cooper, the third Earl of Shaftesbury; but they were aside from the main stream of science, and of common sense. Hobbes was in it. But his clear perception of the situation wrongly viewed was, with the phantasm, probably the decisive impetus down the declivity.

John Locke, without really meaning to, helps fix the modern idea of substance on a stuff of which things are made, underlying all qualities; and, without himself giving up the belief, did the most to make substance (in this sense) disreputable in one phrase when he gave it its name as the "something I know not what." The interpretation of this he carries off from the reputableness of Anaximander's "boundless" with the often-quoted rest of the passage about the "Indian" and what the earth rests on—a fine phrase and a fine story (from a somewhat unexpected phrase-maker and story-teller) which finely test and put into suspicion the literal and existential acceptability of a stuff theory when pushed. We feel the attractiveness of the apple. That rests, partly, on the color, which we see. The color may rest on the shape and motion; and these perhaps on the corpuscular nature, the "real essence" for Locke; and so to some more arcane presence. And this "rests on"?—"Something I know not what" and "You must not ask that." So the honest and common-sense English semanticist tries to weigh the ghost of the abstraction of Anaximander's boundless and Aristotle's substrate rematerialized for the physics of Descartes. He does not like the result but sees no way to avoid the regress or to deny that in which all perceived and all theorized characters inhere.

What is often not remembered in this connection is that when, as in talking of "power," he comes to Aristotle's doctrine of things as changing, doing, and being done to, Locke is not only willing to go along, but glad to. And he goes along in passages much longer and more varied than those he gave to his dilemma with what he thought of as "substance."

The layer-by-layer procedure toward substance we have used above—from value to color to shape to corpuscle to X to x—is the one suggested by the story of the Indian and his successive resting-grounds for the earth. But it is not the procedure of Locke's own trouble with "substance," which is rather a procedure of moving around a thing and plucking off all its discoverable characters, one after another, but all as it were on the same level—and then wondering what could be, although it must be, left. Descartes tells us precisely what is left, what must be there to start with and to end with, as matter: in the language of Francis Bacon, a precisely formed, though naked, Cupid. The layer-by-layer procedure takes us to Anaximander and Aristotle and the necessary but never actual substrate, a completely formless Cupid. Bacon's own "body," and I think Hobbes's, like the Milesian and Aristotle's living body, is more richly, but imprecisely, more "potentially" clothed than Descartes'.

Locke's warmth of feeling for power, as for resistance (which ranks first for him among the "primary qualities," where Descartes and the Continentals do not want it at all), shows Locke's nearness in the English tradition of Milesian body and qualitative motion as against the Cartesian geometrical matter and motion. This is also shown in his long argument with Edward Stillingfleet, the Bishop of Worcester, as to whether God can give matter the power of consciousness. Along with Aristotle's actual existing matter and even its simplest "yearning for form as the female yearns for the male," or Hobbes's "appetency," surely even Locke's God —not the most supralogically omnipotent—can quite easily mold or allow a thinking thing. But with a strict atomic or Cartesian matter precisely defined as including only size-shape-position-motion and as excluding responsiveness, the job becomes one for a fiat-out-of-nothing, which would not make matter think but add thinking to matter à la Descartes, or for a supralogical omnipotence.

Also without really meaning to, John Locke gave us our modern, distinct—if not at all clear—idea of the idea, taking Hobbes's phantasm literally and seriously as he did everything. He also took Hobbes's "all knowledge comes from the phantasm," took it seriously and completely, and turned it into his own maxim (the maxim of the world since): "All knowledge comes from experience." His early draft of that so-called bible of the eighteenth century, the *Essay on the Human Understanding*, shows that Locke's first understanding of the nature of perceiving the world is much more realistic than his final one: the phantasms, the "ideas," involved a saving remnant, an ingredient, of direct apprehension, grasp, contemplative possession of what is perceived but is apart from the perceiving. The primary qualities are not only in the thing but are directly perceived and not "phantasmally" reproduced "in" the mind; they are also, as it were, embroidered with all the secondary qualities as well as feelings. I think this is indeed the paradigm of the general theory of perception of Locke's modern predecessors and a sort of continuation, through the medieval "sensible species," of Aristotle's theory that when we perceive, the form but not the matter of the thing perceived is received into the psyche. By the seventeenth century "form," with its proper antecedent Pythagorean association of "figure," has come to focus in shape, in the geometric and arithmetic. This is made express and emphatic as a hypothesis about perception in that second part of Descartes's *Direction of the Mind* after Descartes consents to become understandable by the use of the shape hypothesis. And more epistemologically it is (and explains) what Descartes means by "formal" truth as more than merely "objective" truth of idea. So when Descartes tells us,

> The perceptions of the senses are related simply to the intimate union which exists between body and mind, and . . . while by their means we are made aware of what in external bodies can profit or hurt this union, they do not present them

to us as they are in themselves unless occasionally and accidentally. . . . In this way we shall ascertain that the nature of matter or body in its universal aspect consists . . . solely in the fact that it is a substance extended in length, breadth and depth. . . . [*Principles*, II, iii, iv]

he does not mean that the senses pick out from the richness of the real what is hurtful or profitable, but that they put into the soul qualitative symbols of the threats or promises of the outside; while the "formal" truth with respect to that outside material world can be found in the senses only by paring away and simplifying, with intellectual scrutiny, down to that extension which is univocally both in the matter of the world and in our perception.

The Englishmen, Bacon and Hobbes, kept this assurance of formal realism plus a suspiciousness of the Continental abstractions and an assurance that even the nonformal elements in perception and sensation are not a phenomenal or differently existing mental-content world but are themselves endeavors and appetencies in bodily but living nature. Locke had something of this bodiliness; but he had taken Hobbes's phantasm seriously. He announces at once (*Essay*, Introduction, § 8) that "idea" means "phantasm," or "whatsoever is the object of the understanding when as man thinks" (a permissible nominal definition except for the reminder that "object" still then meant not thing but presentation), and then, casting the die in a sentence I should vigorously *not* grant, "I presume it will be easily granted me, that there are such ideas *in men's minds*" (italics mine). By the time Locke wrote this sentence he had evidently drawn into the mind all that we directly sense, however much some aspects of it may "resemble" what is beyond. If, indeed, the "object" is a composite of externally real and internally subjective items, as for example of shape and color, how is it, he seems to have asked himself, that the two items never get unpasted? Even our 1968 movies, put together by several projectors, require a crew of watchful technicians and then sometimes lose single focus. And our movie projections are of the same sort in their physics; our knowing would be a superposition of ontologically different natures. The honest Locke was no fighter with the preposterous. Let there be a picture in the mind, a stream of ideas; and let the mind do the best it may—and Locke is modestly quite confident of doing quite well enough with our "candle"—to know what it needs to know about itself and the world around it. After a little, in the ingenuity of philosophic history—which is often not at all averse to the task of making the preposterous intelligible—the mind and the world are both going to collapse into the picture.

Such a story is the answer to the possible question as to why a study of substance should be excited about the theory of perception. As the theory of perception becomes phantasmal, the subjective becomes picturesque and objective in seeming, and the known presence and the theoretic axiom of the subject, the self, is forgotten. And as the theory of perception becomes phantasmal, the world is left in need of argument, argument is not enough, and the world becomes phantasmal. So, as now, substance becomes unfashionable. And so, as now, philosophy becomes at best fashionable, and usually out of touch with common sense and common patience.

George Berkeley was willing, with his own imaginative aims and interpretation, to be persuaded of Locke's "way of ideas" for all the "objects of knowledge." But he saved himself from its subjectivistic and antisubstantialist tendency by his warm assurance of the reality of the self, of spirit, and of God. This enabled him to stress his early advocacy of what seemed to him, and what doubtless was for the time, his most original doctrine: the nonexistence of "unthinking matter." This even lets him outmaneuver the subjectivity of the idea, for from his firm base of spirit he can assert the idea as what it is in its own vivid presence, and without demeaning it as the "mere representation" of anything—except the language and grace of God. So of supposed things like chairs and mountains he can repeatedly declare "their *esse* is *percipi*," their being is to be perceived; for them, to be means to be in some mind's acquaintance. But Berkeley never says, and never would have been able to imagine himself being brought to say, "*esse* is *percipi*." All activity is of spirit, and true being is active; perceiving itself is an activity, and what is perceived, the "object," is inactive, dependent upon the perceiving subject. On the first page of the *Principles of Human Knowledge* we are told that "all the objects of knowledge are idea." On the second we are told that in addition to the objects of knowledge there is that which knows, the subject of knowing, the self, the soul, spirit. Of selves it is not true that their being is *percipi*; it is not even *percipere*. Their *esse* is simply *esse*, substantial existence, the root meaning of *esse*; although our souls' *esse* is not original since we owe our existence to God.

That our ideas, although not real in the way we are, have a reality for Berkeley, is a fact of which students, and teachers, have every now and then to be reminded. The distinction between the real and the subjective has been, I think, for common sense usually between the world which we sense and perhaps otherwise perceive outside and the internal stomach aches or emotional responses which our physiological and psychological internalities add to our perceiving. When the subjective addition moves in on the apparently external object, as it does in seventeenth-century theory as I have taken it, the line becomes more difficult to place but the distinction remains the same: between what we truly "see" and what we add. When we find ourselves in Locke's completed dualism, all that we are aware of is subjective and the real world has withdrawn beyond our acquaintance but not beyond our belief. One way to drop contrariety is to deny the contrary. Berkeley, declaring there is no unthinking material thing, takes away the reproach of the idea as a flimsy substitute for the thing. It is no longer less real as subjective, not material; it is less real as unsubstantial, less real than spirit.

So when the farmer sees a round red apple on his tree, bites it, and finds it cool and juicy and sweet and refreshing to taste and smell and energy, Berkeley waves aside the zealous scientist who would tell the farmer the real apple is an atomic configuration without color or taste, imperceptible and literally unimaginable. Berkeley assures us, and the farmer, that the apple is just as the farmer sees and tastes—especially if the farmer has the childlike recognition of the glory of God in God's language of the senses and nature. Berkeley is quite honest—if somewhat poetically kind to common-sense religion and religious common sense—when he calls himself the champion of common sense as well as of religion. He thought seventeenth-century science and philosophy had stolen the rich and lovely and meaningful world that our senses know and substituted an abstract mathematical machine, and this machine then gets between us and our God.

For our ideas of the world, or rather our ideas which are the world, although they are not representative and bring us no messages of a senseless world behind them, are communicative and syntactic. They make a descriptively and narratively consistent world for each of us and a common world for all of us. That a ball should both look and feel round and should appear round to several is scarcely a marvel; but that visual roundess and tangible roundness should associate themselves for one and for many is a marvel, and a marvel that Berkeley welcomes; for it is the marvel of the syntactic language of the creative and infinite spirit with his creatures. The meaningfulness of human language is one of the most trustworthy assurances of the presence of another person, as indeed is the diminishingly syntactic communication of the animal. So Berkeley is assured (but not only so) of the presence of God.

But all this beauty and meaning of the ideas goes with their fragile inactivity and "object of knowledge" character. They do nothing, and they lapse without the activity of the mind that has them. And they do never and can never represent, stand for, anything of which they are images. So far as I can see, for Berkeley (and here I agree) there literally are no literal mental images—Pompey's statua was an image of Pompey but it was not in Mark Antony's mind when he spoke in the Forum. Ideas have no substance and they stand for no substance. So, for all his enthusiasm and affection for the ideas as his own, Berkeley is quickly aware he can have no idea of himself or of self. If he had found such an idea he would have been scandalized for, on the basis of his own prized theory and belief, it would have meant that he himself was nothing but an idea and that he would lapse and cease and not be if he stopped holding that idea. I suppose he might be for someone else—that is he might be among someone else's ideas since there could be no more real self—if that idea happened to pop up there. And it seems our very use of that pronoun "he" for George Berkeley —the fact of our never falling into the curious dilemma of having to choose between using the pronoun for the ideas which are *him* or using *it* for our idea of *him*, and then of deciding whether our idea of him is our idea of the ideas which are him or our idea of the ideas we have when we look at him, and whether those ideas are our visual ideas of his body or what—yes, it seems all this ought to put us on his side. Selves there are and no self is a sight, a sound, a touch, a taste, a smell, or any assemblage of these in some mind. There is no idea, in Berkeley's sense, of self.

Hume had no such sensibility. I think he was silly to say he could find no idea or "impression" of the self and so he would not believe the self is real. He learned so much from Berkeley; why did he not learn that if he were to find himself among his impressions and ideas, he could have it nowhere else? I suppose the answer for Hume is that he never really believed the theory of ideas that Berkeley so warmly believed, although he verbally accepted it as a part of his intellectual skepticism (whereas Berkeley made it part of his intellectual and esthetic faith). And the answer for Hume is also that his is a two-level doctrine with his skepticism as a sort of avowedly hypocritical front for his assurance of the propensities of "human nature." On this basis the writers since Hume, who often ignore his skepticism as to his skepticism and his realism as to the passions, are still sillier when they assert that Hume merely said what Berkeley should have said.

To be sure the knowledge of the self makes a problem, as Berkeley is aware. If not an "object of knowledge," the self is still something we talk about, a topic of discourse, and the ground or subject of our objects and known both intuitively and as necessary. Let us call its presence to our minds a "notion," not idea. The difference? It is not as vanishing as some funmakers suppose. The idea is like a picture, an image, the "phantasm." The notion we cannot figure. It may be like that recognition of activity which as Spinoza tells us, or tries to tell us, at the end of the second book of the *Ethics*, is more needful to the mind than the easier images and words. And Berkeley soon comes to know what the rest of his century did not have the wit, honesty, or insight to heed or understand, except in part and at cross-purposes: Self is not the only notion or only important notion. Of cause, Berkeley says briefly but clearly what Hume then said at length: we do not see, hear, touch, taste, or smell it. Yet, says Berkeley, we use it and believe it and indeed are acquainted with it. So, more controversially, of the physicist's "force," the preacher's "grace." Relations generally, Berkeley says, are notional, since in order to "imagine" one we have arbitrarily to supply two or more terms and then understand what we mean. Is this not true also of the master value word, "good"? What is your "idea" of good, not of this or that of the many good things we know but of good? Yet we all know good, or we would not know that those good things are good—even when it turns out, or should turn out, that we were mistaken.

Thus Berkeley's strictly nonrepresentative ideas required his substantialism, for him at least, and strengthened his substantialism with regard to himself, other selves, and God; and at the same time taught him that knowing is more than any presence of, or even awareness of, ideas. His love of the ideas enabled him to be clear as to their shortcoming as well as their beauty and reality; and his profoundly enriched knowledge of knowing enabled him to feel at home with the substances and the active realities of the world we live in, which are not "objects of knowledge" as the ideas are. I do not want his "idealism." I get too many intellectual as well as bodily comforts from body. I have come all the way from impatience with Dr. Johnson when he kicked the stone in the road to thinking he had the best answer to Dr. Berkeley. It is true that if I admit the "objects of knowledge" as "ideas," as psychological objects "in the mind," then I will go on as far as Berkeley went and stop where he stopped. But I prefer to stop before his step among the ideas, to refuse all ideas. There is nothing in my mind but minding and that is an activity of the self which is just what it may turn out to be—apparently a body that is responsive, an awareness that chooses and loves, a substance that maintains itself through constant change.

The misfortune is that the newest and most profound aspect of Berkeley, his partly grasped or expounded theory of knowledge beyond the idea, was not understood and not taken up; and the oldest aspect, his common-sense realism as to the qualities of things and as to the existence of the self, was promptly shoved aside by the ingenuities of Hume and phenomenalism and "absolute idealism"; while that for which his youthful enthusiasm excusably burned, his immaterialism, went to encourage and divert the ingenuity which was ignoring and destroying the worthwhile parts of his doctrine and his belief.

Berkeley might have been a restorer of the notion of substance. He is a figure in its caricaturization. With Shaftesbury he is the imagination of the age. And Shaftesbury, who might have understood or who indeed may have dimly anticipated the view of knowing most nearly set forth in the seventh dialogue of *Alciphron*, died young and now figures ironically as the free-thinker opponent of Berkeley's polemic, Alciphron himself, in that work—at once perhaps Berkeley's most profound work and certainly the one in which his ecclesiasticism shows. But the age went off after the sedater side of Locke, the correctness of Pope, and the wit of Hume's false front; so that when imagination and depth came back in the later century it had to be rebellious and violent.

David Hume completes the retraction of the realistic entities of common-sense belief—the knowing selves and the known things—into that at best half-realistic device the mental content, the phantasm, the idea, which was made up or discovered (somewhat late in the story) to help account for the selves' mistakes about present things and their successes with absent things, as it had first, I suppose, helped account for the selves' dreams. So now there are "loose and disconnected" impressions and ideas—not only nonrepresentative, as were Berkeley's ideas, but also nonpresentative since there is no self to be presented to. They are "conscious ideas" although it hardly seems they are conscious of themselves (certainly not "reflectively" so) or of each other. Since our "ontological argument for the existence of substance" proves there must be a "most really there," these ideas, or, in the Lockean and more recent generalization, experience, is or are substance. They meet the criterion of relative, or even absolute, independence since there is nothing else; and they could be developed into a phantasmal Spinozism with an infinite number of intra-experiential aspects or attributes known and unknown, or Leibnizianly into a pre-established harmony of idea-monads. Their supposed fleetingness introduces a difficulty here, as does relative endurance for the criterion of substance; but the phenomenalist may say, if he wishes, that the only thing that endures at all is the species phenomena or, as later and more realistically and imaginatively with Whitehead, he may thread his experiences together into "societies," individuals by "prehension." Actually, it is hard to think of anything more unlike a monad than an idea; and anyone who tries to make his substance of ideas must do without that unique character prized by the Aristotelian substantialist—the focusing of the individual mind.

Hume evidently enjoyed his virtuosity but never believed its theoretic outcome. His language—as he tells us but only inadequately—is often realistic in even its least realistic topics. In the second part of the *Treatise* (the *Enquiries* are more common-sense in manner), on "The Passions," almost no effort is made to keep the impression-idea metaphysics. The passions, we are told on the first page, are "impressions," "secondary impressions" (we are referred back to the "reflective impressions" of the first book—a rather curious offshoot of Locke's "reflective ideas"); but to be bothered about the background of these passions would take us at once into "anatomy and natural philosophy." Anatomy and physiology are not forbidden words or topics to the Humean phenomenalist, but they are not the underlying origin of anything. Hume has given us the key to all this in the title for this first and most incisive of his books: *A Treatise of Human Nature.* The first part alone deals with the understanding: "The reason is and of a right ought to be the slave of the passions." The second and third books of the *Treatise* have to do with the passions and with morals (which are not "rational"), and these are more important, and more real, in human nature. The understanding leaves us somewhat skeptical skeptics, but the understanding should mind its own business, and when we "leave our closet" we go to the coffee house and our friends and we believe and act as they do, according to the propensities of human nature —with, to be sure, an enlightened moral sentiment, sympathy, and a decent recognition of the entertainment of polite society and the dangers of "delusive superstition."

Hume does not assert an ontology of emotion or will— except, as it were, pragmatically. Such an ontology may be suggested in his unargued assurance that human nature is the same everywhere and is so not in its logic but in its feelings. And it may be suggested in his assurance that the understanding is as such and utterly inefficacious. This view, that it is not enough—not even partly enough—to know unless in addition there be a "motive," is one that seems quite foreign to common sense and early theory; but it is one that appears every now and then after the third book of

Aristotle's *De anima* and becomes orthodox and even ax-iomatic in modern philosophy. It is emphatic in Spinoza, for all his apparent anticipation of something like Berkeley's doctrine of the activity essential in knowing and also in the object known. Hume makes it still more emphatic and more axiomatic.

In basis it is presumably a particular, and I think a particularly unfortunate, working of that process we have noticed a number of times whereby the elements we come to in our analysis are assumed to be original components of what we have been analyzing. Looking back we can see at least a physical analogue in Empedocles' separation of motion and force; and we may find a hint of it in the *Republic* in the need the philosopher kings have of the "defense establishment" guardians to keep the productive class in line with the directions of wisdom. Much more operative in the development of the doctrine that knowledge is "perfectly inert" in respect of the knower's action—as Hume says of the "understanding"—is the corresponding division of the soul into the reason, the spirited part, and the appetites. (Both divisions—of the citizens and of the soul of the single citizen—come down from the Pythagorean metaphor of the three sorts of the Olympic games: those who take care of the crowd and the arrangements, those who compete, those who look on and understand.)

Going from the three classes of the state to the three parts of the soul, the fundamental fallacy of that fine and sometimes useful analogy gets in its counterdamage. Its direct damage is to the members of the state: for, though an abstracted aspect or activity of the soul can scarcely complain if it is not supposed to do what it is not supposed to do, anymore than the number two complains that its definition does not let it be an odd number, the individual human being who happens to be a citizen and happens to be good at making speeches, like Winston Churchill, will have a perfectly good complaint if he is told he must not also paint pictures.

In the counter direction, the individual human beings who are citizens are separate and varyingly separable, are born and move and grow and die separately. The classes, any classes, seem to me to be contrivances on partly arbitrary and abstract grounds, but even they can be taken as collections and thought of as herded into separate enclosures. There are no such parts of the soul. However we contrive a division, it has been and may be divided differently. We can set up a part of the soul we call "reason" or "understanding" or "knowledge" and define it as being "cognitive" and only cognitive; and then "it" can never be anything else. But it may be the case, and I am persuaded is the case, that no actual instance of my knowing, my cognition, or yours, or any other person's, ever exists without growing out of and into action—not only action of the knower but also ordinarily action of the object known—and without involving feeling, value, and possible choice. So when we abstractly define knowledge as a part of the soul and say that when an actual person knows he must call in feeling, Aristotle's inclination, Hume's propension, we are calling for what the abstraction, when it exists, guarantees. It guarantees this because what we have chosen to abstract our aspective knowing (or whatever) from was all that other and was so substantially: neither nature nor God put the substance together out of those elements. I think also that if our abstracting and defining is accurately and successfully done it will be so far from debarring participation of the parts of the soul that the definitions of the parts will exhibit the internal relations that allow us to infer the intervention of the other parts.

But it was only the master analytic scalpel of Aristotle

that laid out psychologically the doings of the soul and, especially for our present interest, the need on the part of animal motion—which Plato had been content to leave just as the contribution of soul—for something more than those abilities of the nutritive, the sensitive, and the rational souls which the first two books of the *De anima* had worked out: chiefly the five senses, the "common sense," and thinking with the passive and the active reason. So this last book of the *De anima* seems to give us both the idea as image and the inertness of knowledge-without-inclination; and indeed, also perhaps in this last, the seed of the soon-after invention of the will, which the Greeks previously seem, sufficiently happily, to have done without.

The shredding of our conscious life (the soul) into knowledge plus feeling plus impulse (normal but unemphasized from the time of Aristotle on) was accelerated with the analysis of modern science and philosophy. The process went on to shred impulse—propensity—into many "motives" among the intellectualist phenomenalists, and, among the more biologically inclined of the later nineteenth and early twentieth centuries, into many instincts (the word was just beginning to appear in modern use, or something like modern use, in the later eighteenth century, for example with Gibbon and Burke). The motive development, going back to Locke and indeed to Hobbes with their analysis of "deliberation," was helped by and itself greatly helped the growing psychological determinism. Whatever one does can be said to be the outcome of whatever motive or motives may be needed to produce it, regardless of the doer's unawareness of those motives. "Motive" here was apt to be that part of the total intention (the prevision of the action and its consequences) which fits in with an underlying passional propensity to propel action. Thus the needful dynamic may be felt to be in the underlying propensity rather than in the more particular and particularizing part of the intention which the dynamic seizes upon as its target.

This associates the motive doctrine with the later fashionable "instinct" development—which similarly buttressed determinism in a more bodily interpretation. Whatever one does can be said to be the outcome of the appropriate instinct, an unlearned and inexplicable but by no means altogether blind or useless mode of performance. It has been counted up that by 1930 a total of some 3,000 instincts proposed by psychologists was in the field; and it is clear that this number did much to aid the attack which was now being led by the behaviorists against the notion, or at least against the word.

I have been fond of claiming some credit for that attack. The founder of behaviorism, John Broadus Watson, and my teacher of philosophy, Arthur Lovejoy, gave a joint seminar which was a model of its sort—one year using a still-unpublished manuscript of Bertrand Russell's *The Analysis of Mind*. Lovejoy and Watson, disagreeing widely and radically, were brilliant arguers who had the rare ability to argue without disputing; to be ferocious without losing their tempers; not to sulk. One day I was reporting as a student in the seminar and used the phrase "intelligent action." Watson interposed that he did not doubt I knew what it meant but he did not, that for him all action was instinctive or habitual. Retorting with, I think, mainly verbal dexterity, I said I did not doubt he knew what "instinctive action" meant but I did not; for me all action was intelligent or habitual. He laughed and I went on with my report. The next week he came in and at once told us he still wanted no muddling with intelligent action *but* (he was always generous with the individual student, certainly with me) he had decided I was right about instinct—it was even worse—and he would settle for random, reflex, and habitual (conditioned reflex). It is history that he and his behaviorists became the front of the widely successful battle against instinct. Instinct is now making a comeback, in chastened form, with the ethologists. For my part I willingly accepted the random while hanging on to the intelligent. Looking over his *Behaviorism* again, I can see I also accepted some of his theory and tactics, for I have often said that the rocking chair rocks without our calling in a rocking instinct to explain it. The image is not his, but the appeal to physical structure is. I added, as he would not have added, that our superiority in intelligence, awareness, over the chair lets us see that the functioning of structure is fun and lets us try and sometimes succeed in finding new ways and sometimes fail or lamentably go astray.

Scarcely were instincts subdued, to be sure, when they began to be replaced with "drives." There was a bit of the same multiplication; but something had been learned, not only from the behaviorists. At the present time, it seems to me, the lively, scientifically based and qualified study of motivation can compliment itself—as can other fields—that psychology has found depth without myth in the move toward the one motive: motivation; living things are active. This is human nature because it is animal nature, is biological nature, or indeed perhaps is nature.

Is there more specific human nature? For my part, as I said in parting from and in support of Watson, I should be content to say we have a wider and brighter field of awareness than the plants and the other animals; and we are, for example, two-legged, which makes human nature different from dog nature, and featherless, which makes human nature different from chicken nature. We aspire and we get tired. So in its range does every living thing. We are vain, anxious for our own and others' applause (Lovejoy's "approbativeness"), and foolish; susceptible to fear and cowardice, selfishness, cruelty, and deceit, but also capable of their opposites. So in his range is every animal. And these characters not merely are so, they must be so in the nature of life as aware and choosing (as Socrates may be said to have seen); just as it must be the character of a circle to be the figure of maximum enclosure.

In my days of teaching aesthetics I argued that the artist, creative or performing, may have emotion as a topic (there are other topics) and may express emotion in the sense that the mathematician expresses the binomial theorem when he writes its symbols. But if the artist expresses the emotion as the hurt animal—dog or human—expresses his pain, then it is not art or not good art; it may be sentimentalized art, even very skillfully artful; still a special but frequent sort of bad art.

John Stuart Mill said motives have nothing to do with the good or bad of action (although much to do with the good or bad of the agent). It may be that insofar as action is "motivated" it is not virtue. The supposed psychological causation from the particular dynamic instinct, drive, impulse (if any), or from that particular item or extent of the intention which is the agent's target, will be a matter of determinable or indeterminable fact. The goodness of the person might be in the goodness of his motives or his choices, and the goodness of the act might be in conformity to principle or acceptability of outcome. That beautifully two-handled word "virtue" looks both ways, it seems: with something of the Greek "arete" for the skill with which the good workman brings about his end in view and something also of the Greek "practical wisdom" which chooses—as Aristotle says in the *Rhetoric*—what the man who knows most about it would choose, if he is a good man. Or shall we say that action, like music, should stand wisely in the light of relevant emotion and desire but should not be driven by it, should not be apart from the life from which it springs yet should not be its outburst? But the virtuous man has a harder job than the good musician: for the musician can or must, at his peril, sacrifice some other goods to his music. The man, with his widest and by definition final end, must choose among often competing ends and cannot take refuge in the supposition that any abstraction of virtue-as-such or good-as-such may itself be taken as a specific target.

We can and should say that the good man has the better of it as against the bad man. But we must quickly add that if we do right for this reason—as a motive—we do not do right. So the virtue of motive, requisite when generalized to the proper degree, can be made a reason, but a hypocritical one which is worse than the direct impulse.

Luke, in the chapter that includes the parable of the talents, starts off by warning that we must be better than the publicans who "have their reward"; and winds up, in his own superb narrative fashion, but not always easily logical fashion, urging us to be good for the sake of the goods "pressed down and running over" that the good shall get. So our substitute preacher read the whole chapter, forgot the precious beginning, and eloquently proceeded to try to bribe us into righteousness.

This too is substance: the integralness of life, knowledge, love, choice; Aristotle's "contrary predicates" and Heraclitus' fire, folly, and "the common."

Substance "is what has external relations and the parts of which have external relations." Square is a species of rectangle as red is of color. Straight is contrary of crooked. Justice resembles courage as against deceit. But Solomon was the son of David and one of his hands was right and one left. Solomon was a substance—or existed, for an existent collection which may not be a substance (say David's army) also has external relations; and the part which may not be a substance (say the surface of Solomon's body) has external relations even if no parts. But these are substantial.

Taking Locke's thesis that only the perception of the agreement and disagreement of our ideas (internal relations) is knowledge, and Berkeley's thesis that cause (an old-time master external relation) is never observable, Hume can figure as the somewhat surprising champion of internal relations (such as are left) and destroyer of external relations. But what of passion? Is it internal or external? It is human nature, and Humean human nature, which is most internal; but it is trustworthily uniform and it governs our dealings with the outside as well as our belief about the outside. "Reason the card, but passion is the gale." Thus human nature, as a radically accepted set of biases and propensions and certainly not as a searchlight power upon the world plus an observable anatomy, becomes the governor of action and judgment.

CHAPTER V

PHENOMENALISM AND POSTPHENOMENALISM

David Hume thought he knew much more about human nature than that it knows what there is to know and that it has two legs and lungs; though he knows it less rationally. He knew human nature as a shrewd and enlightened observer. How he knew it was the same in China as in London, Edinburgh, and Paris he does not tell us. I suppose he would say, not having read Watson on infants and learning—or Ruth Benedict on cultural relativity—why not the same? That understanding can have no direct effect on action he knows more rationally: by definition or axiomatically (despite his careful but to me question-begging argument in the *Treatise*, II,iii,3). The products of analysis, factual and logical, are final, except for the recognition that more analysis may come. And "all coherence is lost"; except for the fact that among human propensities is the propensity toward an idea of coherence and so toward a belief in some substance or substantiality, even a belief in our own.

If we take Hume's propensities and make them rational, and his uniformitarianism and make it necessary; call our fond believing human nature the forms and categories of sensibility and understanding, of mind as such; then we have Immanuel Kant. Surely the two men are contrasts, as are their languages and manners of argument; yet their basic theories—perhaps as I interpret them without full sympathy for either—rather invite a transformation equation. And Kant may be said to formalize and clarify the splitting in the approach to substance which was apparent in Locke but undeveloped; which was shunned by Berkeley; and which was made inescapable in the reduction of all things to phenomena in the theoretical theory of Hume. There had been two chief directions in which men had looked for substance: Is what is really there individual things, or an underlying stuff? Now with "the way of ideas": Is substance real-beyond-knowledge or is it an idea? The first alternatives appear in Locke's two treatments of substance under the rubric of power and as the "something I know not what." But it can also be seen that the latter treatment, the substrate, leaves Locke reluctantly accepting the idea of substance as needed by his other ideas and by their dialectical use together (the Kantian method); the former, power, takes him at once into that independent world of resistant things which he never gave up. Berkeley made substance spirit but kept it individual and independent; and he limited ideas to the picturesque "objects of knowledge." Thus selves—and cause—are not ideas nor can there be ideas of them. For Hume there is and can be, for our philosophic understanding, nothing but ideas ("impressions and ideas"); so "substance" as a topic of discourse without a proper impression must be philosophically a myth, which nevertheless our human nature inclines us to act upon and talk of believingly.

For Kant substance is the "first analogy"; cause is the second analogy. This at first sounds to me profoundly silly: the most real, and the next-to-most real, facts of existence being presented as abstract hypotheses needful for the working of a calculus. But I know it is not silly (it may in a sense be profoundly superficial); it is one of many instances but a privileged instance of Kant's amazing combination of honesty and accuracy with ingeniously pedantic loyalty to the premises he has started with. Hume, Kant is saying, is right in that experience is phenomenal and the sensation in experience is phantasmal and unstructured. But we do know and Newton is to be trusted. So it must be that the forms of our knowledge, whereby experience has structure and science is possible and trustworthy, are necessary in the minding of mind—not only requisite for knowledge but sure in knowing. So the dialectic of knowledge reaches out for "substance"—the idea, the form, the category, the first analogy—without caring whether substantial substance is or not. But Kant cares; and so we have—to the dismay of some—the "thing in itself."

The "analogies of experience," the specifications of the category of relation, in one way are derived from the logician's classification of propositions as categorical, hypothetical, alternative: the first analogy, substance, being the categorical *This is thus;* the second analogy, cause, being the hypothetical *If this is thus then that is so.* This is a sagacious and plausible way to get at the twelve forms the understanding works with—and distinctive of the difference between Kant and Hume. I have come to think it is true and important that the mind naturally, and the scientist's mind almost inevitably, tends to see what has happened in terms of antecedents. But I think it is more basically true and important that cause is real and effective but far from all-embracing: there are also chance and freedom. These views I had come to without thought of Kant. Then I became aware that they are an easy transformation from Kant's doctrine that the second analogy is all-embracing within experience but that the *noumenal egos* are free and the things-in-themselves are at least not phenomena under the dialectical command of the second analogy. But I can do without all phenomena and let the habits of people and scientists be just that; and it seems to be so much better to let the things-in-themselves and the selves-in-themselves be the ones we started life with and still know best and most directly.

Kant's celebrated rebuttal of the ontological argument

for the existence of God suggests itself for redeployment against Kant's own thing in itself and against my suggested variation of the ontological argument for substance. Existence being a part of the meaning of the "concept" of God, says Kant, it follows that when we think of God we must think of him as existing, but it does not follow that he exists —substantially. I would not want to change anything of the superb simplicity and eloquence of Anselm's putting of his argument in the encounter with the Biblical "fool" who "says in his heart"; but, in the light of the long subsequent argument over the argument, it seems unfortunate that Anselm began with that thinking in the heart, and perhaps more unfortunate that his *cogitari* became the then new-fangled "conceived" and so "concept." An "ontological argument for existence" has to start from what is thought and try to go to what exists; and I suspect that without some ingredient of existence it cannot succeed; but it does not have to start with an actual mental content, an idea or a concept. Yet if I am allowed to consider the supposed presence of this idea and what it is supposed to be—if I am allowed to think about it and not merely to have it or, in the Humean sense, be it—then I can say, "If this poor beautiful thing is all there is, then it is by definition substance; but I know it is not all, for there is this I, or at least this thinking, which thinks about it"; and I can also say as Kant says in this section of the first *Critique* on the division of all things into *phenomena* and *noumena* that there is a clear insufficiency in the nature of the idea for independent being. Before Descartes' "I think therefore I am," he should have declared "I think, therefore there is something to think about." But this, while I believe it would have taken him beyond the realm of post-Lockean ideas, would not have given him the personal and physical world he wanted.

Arthur Schopenhauer and Friedrich Nietzsche carry on the human-nature-propensity-passion realism-of-the-cellar, which was in David Hume's teaching. They, so far as I know, never say or feel they are carrying on from Hume, and in their nineteenth-century romanticism the passions are more passionate and have become the will, or the Will. In Nietzsche the metaphysical-epistemological interest lapses more and more into the moral, and his moral homiletic, like his personality, can scarcely be thought Humean. The idealism as to matter of Schopenhauer and Nietzsche, and their personalism, are more like Berkeley's (instructors have liked to make it seem that the later Germans derive from Kant, playing the role of Locke to his English successors); but their voluntarism feels to me closer to Hume's background and partly anti-intellectualist existence than to the lyrical and esthetic spiritualism of Berkeley. If there is anti-intellectualism in Berkeley, it is Neoplatonic and mystic; Hume's is skeptical and pragmatic. Schopenhauer here, more than Nietzsche, may have elements of Berkeley. What I am concerned about is that Schopenhauer and Nietzsche do represent the revival of a direct substantialism of the living-doing-suffering persuasion, going back perhaps to the power strain of Locke, if not to the Scotist voluntarism of the fourteenth-century Franciscans. The metaphysics is stated by Schopenhauer. Kant, he says emphatically, was right— if he is rescued from the misinterpretations of Hegel—except for his failure to recognize that the thing in itself is not removed from our acquaintance but is indeed that which is best-known, is closest, is ourselves, is will. And Schopenhauer's ethics, with its essential foundation in sympathy, has its kinship with Hume and the eighteenth century (Schopenhauer is dividedly romantic, Enlightenment, and classicist), although its goal and outcome, still equivocal, are as far from Hume as is Sanscrit. His ethics and sympathy add to his feeling for and our assurance of his substantialism. When he tells us: by all means read Newton and learn the mathematics of gravity, but go to the cathedral and feel the pressure of the stones on the arches, columns, and buttresses and you will know weight better—when he gives us such admonitions to sympathetic interaction, he does better for substance than Descartes does in his definition or Kant in his second analogy.

But voluntaristic substantialism seems cramped, or diluted—in its appeal to both common sense and philosophic theory—by a failure of ancient familiarity in what is meant by "will" and by a lack of the greater imaginative stability of those other abstractive directions leading to matter or soul or even the picturesque ideas. (I think it has some advantages, especially over the ideas, in its appeal to our feeling for power.) What is it that stays through, is permanent, in the unresting will? And it suffers by comparison with knowledge, taken as an action or function rather than as content, because of its lack of individual inwardness and outward awareness. What is it that brings the "blind" will into selfhood or response to the world? At any rate the Schopenhauerian will has had a wide influence but one generally becoming shallower and less substantial.

Bergson may be said to have given it its best channel; but Bergson, by his own account, paid more heed to Schelling (and to Zeno), and his influence in turn has been more epistemological than metaphysical. Schopenhauer we have said was radically moralized by Nietzsche and so by the existentialists who have used Nietzsche, with a further heavy (or fluffy) infusion of subjectivism. Martin Heidegger, at least by declaration, shuns the subjective, and the possible hope for substantialism among the existentialists would seem to be with him. I think he is the best philosopher among them; but it is doubtful if even a sudden vogue would sufficiently pierce his famous opacity to make him a great influence in philosophy or general thought.

Alfred North Whitehead, by usual consent the best metaphysician and the most hospitable of our century, expresses his debt to Bergson (and to Berkeley) and has among his many backgrounds or similarities something of the will and empathy of Schopenhauer. But I believe our chief gratitude to Whitehead should be for his enrichment of our view of knowing and for varied recognitions of the sort of integralism I have been preaching, not for any ontological realism or substantialism. Here it is not only his aloofness from the word "substance" (taken in Locke's "something I know not what" sense and in that of the physicists' and chemists' substrate) but also the subjectivistic commitment of his "experience" metaphysics that stands in the way.

George Santayana liked the word "substance" and its out-there realism, and might have made a substantialism on more classic grounds, but he too let substance lapse into stuff —a Democritean-Epicurean-Lucretian matter—and added an "epiphenomenal" realm of ideas which the elegant and literal Epicurus never thought of and would never have thought of. Perhaps a more traditional or Aristotelian theory of substance may be achieved by the personalists: Brightman, Flewelling, Bertocci, Smith; but they have not made real impact so far.

So I look to the physicists, who, in this mid-twentieth century, are declaring the abstractness, the finality and artifice, of the notion of substrate, together with its Anaximanderian unboundedness of possibility and Aristotelian potentiality when it is taken in the account of the actual. And the novelty in physics—not only in the Copenhagen school but in Max Born, Schrödinger, Eddington—has doubtless aided a kindred openness in the consideration of life in biology and in the ADN enthusiasms of biophysics and biochemistry.

Whitehead makes a notable exposure of the shortcomings of the modern scientific view of substance as stuff, as geometrical matter, whether or not one goes all the way with him in giving up the "fallacy of simple location" (in which he foreshadows Copenhagen physics). He probably did more than any other philosopher to champion a larger and deeper view of our acquaintance—for the infusion of it by quality and feeling and value. And he makes an honest effort for what he thinks of as realism. But his realism seems to me to be always epistemological and not metaphysical. He cannot do better, for he never breaks the net of that Humean-Hegelian retraction of both the knowing person and the known thing into "knowledge." Why, I have sometimes asked, do not the prizefight reporters go on from the naïve account of one man hitting another to a sophisticated doctrine of "hitledge," and then, when the uninstructed see the heavyweights trying to damage one another, the experts can parcel out the mutual and sometimes symmetrical relations of action and passion of the hitledge on display in the ring. Whitehead's "actual occasions" and "prehensions" as well as his "least puff" of experience are still awarenesses. His nearest approach to substance, a substantialist will feel, is in the "eternal objects," entering into or excluded from the actual occasions. This would be a sort of super-Platonism. He does much to get around this complaint and to reconcile me when he says, as he does, that he wants experiencing rather more than experiences. His is meant to be and is a philosophy of process. So I should want mine to be. I am a Heraclitean who believes that all substance is in process and that nothing else is. The substance changes and is permanent through the change and endures and perdures; it is itself but is never mathematically or logically identical at different times. There is no boy who grows or dancer who dances substantially different from the growing boy or the dancing dancer, although the growing boy will later be the full-grown man and the dancer will go to sleep. "It may be a weakness of my metaphysics" but I cannot—and I have tried to try—imagine a substance that is not in process; and it seems to be still more impossible to imagine a process that is not of a substance. Now it might be a Berkeleyan spiritual substance, even a Cartesian purely thinking substance; but it will not be a mere *percipere* or *penser*. And I weary trying to follow the patience and ingenuity of Whitehead trying to make a world: a continuing world of prehending brevities and an extended world of perspectives. I love knowing but I want a knower and what is known. "This horse and this man" seem to be more than their own knowing or experiencing, and certainly they are more than mine. And I have trouble (partly illicit I do not doubt) with the dynamic and the causal, whose good friend Whitehead meant to be, explaining how my prehending or the horse's makes me lose a bet on him or bring into presumably additional prehension his or my children.

Process requires continuance—per-manence—as well as change. Whitehead was fully aware of this and tries to provide for it in prehensions, and personal "societies" of prehensions, which have an interfusion from one to the next: "actual occasions" of greater or less duration but never long. But can this be enough? It seems to make of me a train of communicating cars at best; hardly a vehicle, much less an organism. There are several trains in my process, with occasional cross glances but not couplings serially, and yet all my own. When I go from the classroom to the race track I am still myself—indeed I may be said in going to renew myself—but the "occasions" scarcely coalesce: at the track everything not racing or gambling is erased. And if, back at lecturing, I use a racing illustration, it is no intrusion of track "experience" into that of the lecture but an intellectual reaching out of the lecturer to something outside himself he has known. If there is danger of split personality, I suspect (I am surely no psychiatrist) the danger is in the overly concentrated attention of the man of single interest. Just as common sense thinks my body goes from the University to Pimlico—a changing body "proceeding" across town —so my self, staying myself but always changing, goes through the changing Baltimore to the track, by tradition stand-pat and the scene of speed and upset. One of the basic charms of the track is the way its problems, as apart from those of the university, come to a conclusion and are gone with every race; while the continuing, and triumphing, and defeated, rejoicing and suffering self can move on to a brand new race—solving as he can the problem of another two dollars.

I am aware that much of what I am doing is no more than translating the language of *Process and Reality* into my ordinary idiom. But I am convinced the idiom is easier, not merely because I know it, but because it is easier: it would be easier to learn and use for one who had known neither. And I think it is easier because it is closer to what is really there. It also seems to me to succeed in saying, or partly saying, what the experience language can not say, despite the wonderful width and depth of Whitehead's consideration, his patience, and his ingenuity.

Santayana's normally Epicurean description of substance as atomic matter is itself rather in his realm of "essences" than it is asserted to be "essential" of the literal being of substance. Santayana's assurance of the symbolic character of knowledge is too real to allow such realism to any description of what stands under knowledge in existence. So the classic atom in the void with the atom's size, shape, position, and motion is both not bare enough (using Bacon's fable with respect to "Cupid or the atom")—as asserting of substance descriptive epithets we cannot be sure of—and too bare—as denying of substance other characters and powers beyond our little symbology. This richness of feeling for the stuff of things brings Santayana back into association with the Milesians and Bacon and also forward into association with the differently based "complementarity" of Bohr, de Broglie, Heisenberg. Here are some sentences from Santayana's Herbert Spencer Lecture on "The Unknowable" at Oxford in 1923:

> A point in which he [Spencer] seems to me to have been a true philosopher . . . [is] his belief in a substance which by its secret operation, in infinite modes, kindles experience. . . . Any experience is incidental to animal life and animal passions, which in turn are incidental to the general flux of substance in the world. Appearances and feelings and consciousness itself are in their nature desultory and unsubstantial yet not altogether groundless nor altogether mad, because substance creates and sustains them. . . .

> We need but sharpen our wits, and shake our minds loose from prejudice, trying new categories, until we come nearer the heart of those substantial dynamic objects which confront us in action. This approach need not be a magical divination of their essence, although when the object recognized is a mind like our own, such literal divination is not impossible.

> Human experience is filled full with such appropriate comments on neighboring modes of substance, and with appropriate names and sketches clapped upon events. Among these signs and tokens there are some especially venerable symbols, those same ideas already mentioned of matter, of God, of the natural world, of various persons and passions. These venerable symbols are characters attributed to substance and its modes by the human imagination, after long experience and much puzzled reflection.

What exists is the substance at work, and this substance is never an idea hypostatized. It is prior to all ideas and descriptions of it, the object that, in their rivalry, they are all endeavoring to report truly. . . . But whether we think fit to call substance there matter, and here God, or invent other names, substance will remain what it is, our ideas and appellations will have no power to create it where it is not, or to dislodge or modify it where it is.

As centers of light, jewels seem rather trivial and monotonous. And yet there is an unmistakable spell about these pebbles. . . . They are substances.[1]

But it is also intimated in these passages about substance that Santayana's mind is as convinced of the ideality of the ideas--both of their unsubstantiality and of their contentual presence—as his heart is moved toward substance. So he is a sort of Locke rendered thoroughly skeptical of any proof of the representative accuracy, or even the representative character, of the ideas, which are now "essences": skeptical and saving his assurance of substance only by his acceptance of "animal faith." I suppose this is the counterpart of Locke's "sensible knowledge" of the world, made self-conscious and critical; for Santayana shares Locke's feeling for the dynamics of acquaintance and makes this too self-conscious and much wider. It is one of his virtues that he was one of the chief twentieth-century voices for enriching our modes of acquaintance. The official post-Humean philosophic psychology, he says, must have been the outcome of studying the dictionary, not the mind.[2] But this makes a difficulty for him like that of Berkeley and the "notion." When Santayana thinks of substance he presumably has to think with an "essence," the meaning of "substance"; but no essence is literally representative; and our acquaintance with

1. Clifton Fadiman, ed., *Reading I've Liked* (New York, 1958), pp. 213, 222, 228, 230, 232.
2. George Santayana, *Scepticism and Animal Faith* (New York, 1923), p. 188.

the substantial things and events of the world is existential and participationist rather than a contemplation of essences. So, corresponding with "knowledge," is "animal faith."

In the lecture on Spencer, Santayana grows wary of the epithet Spencer is fond of, "the unknowable," and says that there cannot be anything that is intrinsically unknowable. This is partly his dislike of what he calls "idealism." It is also because of his restriction of the word "knowledge" to the use in "discourse" of always-partly-arbitrary symbols either in dialectic or in sentences about our fellow things, which we are aware of in living interplay, the existence of which our animal faith gives us ground to assert, and the attributes and relations of which we may be said to "know" in our selection of relevant essences to use in our discourse about them. "Knowledge is a salutation, not an embrace." [3]

It may that his brief association with the "critical realists" in their reply to and controversy with the "new realists" (the two volumes of 1912 and 1920) helped deflect the nonassociative and noncontroversialist Santayana to the emphasis upon "essences" and "animal faith" which marked his middle period, especially the first half of the opening volume of his "realms" series, *Scepticism and Animal Faith*. Perhaps more it was because he was then in his middle period; middle age is well skipped by anyone: certainly the philosopher should be able to say "I have been young and now am old"—or not care.

There is always a gentlemanly skepticism in Santayana —skepticism is by nature well-mannered, he says. But when skepticism becomes theoretical and doctrinaire it becomes pedantic and fits the gentlemanly Santayana ("philosophic dandy," Lovejoy called him) only in his brief poses of deliberate theory. And perhaps this was when he wore it. But

3. George Santayana, *Reason in Common Sense* (New York, 1905), p. 77.

his colleagues fixed upon his pose. And he was proud of his essences. (I do not wish to depreciate them. There is—and he helped us to see it—a Platonic element in any acquaintance, no matter how little intellectual, but ready to be discriminated by our minds. But I think I see dogs and mountains, feel stomach aches, have intimations of immortality, choose goods, say prayers: and none of these are essences.) As the declarer of essences, skepticism, and animal faith, he lost what I want to be grateful for, his influence toward an awareness of a richer and more realistic awareness, and toward substance.

But his earlier more existentialist and more substantialist potentiality was not lost or foreclosed; in *The Life of Reason* and the *Three Philosophical Poets* (*The Sense of Beauty* may be a case apart) it survived the rewriting of the former and the writing of the *Realms of Being*, and even came to the surface inside them. After the first part of *Scepticism and Animal Faith*, chapter XIX on "The Belief in Substance" is one of his warmer statements of substantialism. I could have quoted it rather than the lecture on Spencer. (Both were published in 1923.) At the end of that chapter in my first edition I find I wrote: "If he had not worked so hard earlier to turn the outer perceptions into dreams, essences, illusions, he would not now have to keep them so far apart from partnership with his 'voice of hunger' in announcing and describing substances." The reference is to a sentence just above: "Belief in substance, taken transcendentally, as a critic of knowledge must take it [a caveat from the first part of the book], is the most irrational, animal, and primitive of beliefs: it is the voice of hunger." His old-age book, *The Idea of Christ in the Gospels*, which philosophers are apt to bypass, is appropriately an intensification of some themes of his youth with, I believe, almost no projection of his middle age.

From first to last Santayana uses the word "substance" with kindly feeling for the word and notion if not always for the thing. In the chapter on piety in his early *Reason in Religion* he talks of piety toward the universe. "Its extent, its order, its beauty, its cruelty make it quite impressive. If we dramatize its life and conceive its spirit, we are filled with wonder, terror, and amusement, so magnificent is that spirit, so prolific, inexorable, grammatical and dull. . . . Great is this organism of mud and fire, terrible this vast, painful, glorious experiment. Why should we not look at the universe with piety? Is it not our substance?" And in *Dominations and Powers*, published when he was eighty-eight, there is a passage dwelling on the word "substance" which, if less purple, is more kindly.

In the preface to *Scepticism and Animal Faith* George Santayana said:

> There is one point, indeed, in which I am truly sorry not to be able to profit by the guidance of my contemporaries. There is now a great ferment in natural and mathematical philosophy and the times seem ripe for a new system of nature, at once ingenuous and comprehensive, such as has not appeared since the earlier days of Greece. We may soon be all believing in an honest cosmology, comparable with that of Heraclitus, Pythagoras, or Democritus. I wish such scientific systems joy, and if I were competent to follow or to forecast their procedure, I should gladly avail myself of their results, which are bound to be no less picturesque than instructive. But what exists today is so tentative, obscure, and confused by bad philosophy, that there is no knowing what parts may be sound and what parts merely personal and scatter-brained. If I were a mathematician I should no doubt regale myself, if not the reader, with an electric or logistic system of the universe expressed in algebraic symbols. For good or ill, I am an ignorant man, almost a poet, and I can only spread a feast of what everybody knows.

This was in 1923. The most literary of the philosophers and the one with the least personal involvement in science (a character he carefully intimates in his use of the somewhat quaint "natural and mathematical philosophy" for relativity physics and subatomic physics) is one of the perceptive as to the scientific climate and promise. Albert Einstein's two "breakthrough" papers, on relativity and light quanta, were in 1905, and Max Planck's quantum goes back to 1900. Niels Bohr's theory of the discontinuous electron orbits had been achieved, but quantum mechanics—Bohr's complementarity, Max Born's probability, Louis de Broglie's wave-particle, Erwin Schrödinger's and Werner Heisenberg's differing mathematics and similar indeterminacy—still lay ahead, but not far. It was in 1923 that Charles Galton Darwin, in a paper entitled "The wave theory and the quantum theory," wrote the sentence which Max Jammer (in *The Conceptual Development of Quantum Mechanics*) thinks is the first, but unclear, statement of the wave-particle duplicity. Santayana was not in C. G. Darwin's position; but I think he knew something of the "ferment" in the theory of the atom. And he knew Einstein, to whom his (respectful) references are not infrequent. Relativity, indeed, by 1923 had a vogue—by no means an always admiring one —even among the philosophers. A very infrequent writer of papers, I had written one on the theory of relativity. I have no intention of rereading it, but I think it was not all bad and had a point of some relevance. But I was not as perceptive as Santayana. I did not see in 1923 anything of what seems clear to me now, that the first half of our century, the time of Einstein and Bohr—and possibly what comes after—is one of the great periods, and is so on account of its science, ranking with the early period of the Greeks and the early period of the moderns. A great scientific period must, I think, be great in its contribution to philosophy when the philosophers get around to it, especially its contribution to the theory of substance, what is really there;

and normally in its contribution to that meaning of "substance" which is the Milesian problem of "the constitution of matter," the Milesian physics-philosophy of the stuff of which things are made.

Here Einstein gave us a superbly new shaking-up of the pure-Pythagorean doctrine of space-time-number by the stirring-in of non-Euclidean geometry; and Bohr gave us a superbly new shaking-up of Democritean atomism by a stirring-in of probability and hesitation even as to the "inner" character of the "indivisible" particle itself. In both schools there is the common element, quite differently accented and used, of the ineradicable and uncorrectible effect of measuring upon that which is measured. And as the best-known, human, and not unimportantly theoretic, strand of the story is the inability of the older Einstein to accept the somewhat younger Bohr's indeterminacy, thus creating the continuing distress of the two great men, creators, friends, and opponents.

Such a shaking and loosening, with the optionalism of the three geometries and of the two roles of wave and particle, naturally loosens and reinterprets the alternatives philosophy had supposed it had in the theory as to the reality and actuality (or not) and as to the character of the stuff of things. Pythagoras said all is number, and meant it. And yet the "whole" Pythagoras could not mean it because he was a religious teacher, intent on the career of the soul, which by studying the numbers can win salvation and which is in danger of going bad. Numbers do not have that hope or that worry. Even as describers of nature the Pythagoreans had to call on the outside darkness, albeit under their breath, to fill in and give existence to their forms. Back in Ionia, Anaximander had said all is the boundless, a stuff with no form or limits or character. Yet out of this the forms, limits, characters are, without apology, shaken. Democritus, with the aid of the impossible One of Parmenides and with the audacious introduction of empty space, the void, puts together no more than what is needful from Anaximander and Pythagoras. Inside the atom there is no character except indivisibility. Nothing can be shaken out of an atom, precisely because there is nothing (no character) in there and because there is no nothing (no space) in there. Externally the atom has very little—only size, shape, position, motion—but what it has is very precise—mathematical—and all else is very positively ruled out as not there. Nothing can be shaken out of the atom, but a lot of atoms shaken together do, the theory says, eventuate in all the manyness of characters we know—the qualitative, passionate, valuative, cognitive world we live in—and doubtless eventuate in more characters in other worlds or later in this one if we learn more and make more instruments. How this can be, with nothing but atoms and the void so precisely characterized and so definitely denied further character, has always seemed a puzzle to some imaginations. And the void—its literalness and the definiteness of its negativity, like the kindred adjectives of the atom—has been a hindrance as well as a help.

Greek materialism, or atomism if the word be taken vaguely, as the doctrine of a natural world of bodies moving with regular ways in time and space, has been the normal, if not quite unanimous, acceptance of natural science since the pre-Socratic Greeks. Atomism more precisely—as the assertion of indivisible bits of matter, with size, shape, position, motion only, in a void, and with nothing else substantial—has been more frequently denied, qualified, or embroidered, but has remained in its essentials a general basis of physics and chemistry down to our own time.

Aristotle, although he calls the soul the form of the body, "the first entelechy of a body having life naturally within it," declares the Democritean view that an arrangement of atoms can be life or soul preposterous, as is also, he thinks, the indivisibility of the atom, since it must be and is extended and anything extended can be imagined divided; and to this he added a denial of empty space. And Aristotle was the "master of those who know," especially in the later Middle Ages. But atomism went on, through Epicurus and the Epicureans and others, down to Pierre Gassendi the contemporary of Descartes. (Gassendi, like Ralph Cudworth on the other side in England, might have had a larger influence if he had not been so verbose.) Descartes followed Aristotle (he would not like that phrase) in needing a different soul from that of the atomists, in denying the void, and in denying indivisibility—in favor of the dimensionless point, I suppose. Newton and the English, perhaps with some influence from Bacon, preferred "corpuscle" to atom. Dimitri Mendelyeev with his periodic table brought the new atom back to more Pythagorean elegance. And the atom of Ernest Rutherford, with whom Bohr worked and for whom he wrote his theory of the orbits, is the lineal descendant of the atom of Democritus, or of the presumed creator, Democritus' shadowy teacher, Leucippus of Abdera and Miletus. But this is not the place nor am I the person to give a history of scientific matter. It has been given, from a different point of view, by Stephen Toulmin and June Goodfield (Mrs. Toulmin) in *The Architecture of Matter.*

Democritean atomism, with its precisely given atoms and void, is what Francis Bacon calls Cupid naked but shapely. Thales, with his stuff of water, familiar and familiarly rich in potential variety, is Cupid clothed. Aristotle, and back of him Anaximander, with a substrate asserted as without character, is Cupid not only unclothed but formless. (Bacon has a fourth: "Cupid not only cloaked but masked," which I leave out.) Bacon prefers the naked Cupid but he chides Democritus for the shape he gives him. Bacon, indeed, though he too would not like my saying so, is, on my interpretation of the three men, rather Thalesian than Democritean. I would add to Bacon's apologue that Heraclitus does not belong where Bacon puts him, with Thales and Cupid clothed. For Heraclitus makes his substance not the stuff fire but the person, the soul, the spirit of the individual —man or world—which the fire stands for, as the water and earth of the animal "embodies" the fire of his soul. And so Aristotle, for whom the substrate is only at times and after a fashion substantial while "this man or this horse" is prime substance, is only Anaximanderian in his view of stuff; whereas in his substantialism he is rather in the following of Heraclitus.

So in stuff doctrine we can go with Thales, Anaximander, or Democritus. Or we can formalize away from the materiality of stuff toward space-time-number and go with Pythagoras. Or we can integrate to the full individual with Aristotle. Or we can spiritualize away from matter and the physical toward Neoplatonism. In these rubrics Einstein would figure as Pythagorean, Bohr as Anaximanderian (despite Heisenberg's liking for Heraclitus) or, perhaps, in Bohr's beginning in physics, as Democritean. But Einstein and Bohr, as we said, have shaken the rubrics. A Pythagorean cosmos with three geometries may be a super-Pythagoreanism. A boundless into which has been infused a wave-particle probability might have pleased Anaximander. At any rate some rhetorical if not real easing has been given to the puzzle of how all the somethings of our world can come from what is declared not to be those somethings and to be what those somethings are not. We are now less taken back when Aristotle tells us often that prime matter has no character and then tells us (and in the *Physics* of all places) that prime matter has the character of yearning for character as the female yearns for the male.

One fact that seems to come to light in the study of stuff, matter, is that Democritus alone gives us an account of matter which we can both imagine and be intelligible about. (This may be a measure of its inadequacy.) I have heard many persons challenged to make clear what they mean by "soul" but few challenged to make clear what they mean by "matter." For some years I have liked to ask students a question about what Aristotle means by matter and form; and I have been struck by the regularity with which they have their hardest time trying to tell me what Aristotle means, or what they think he means, or indeed what they themselves mean, by matter. Actually, I suppose we have no acquaintance with pure matter. Nor do we with pure soul. As to form, or "Idea," I think we have no existential acquaintance, or "reminiscence," of pure form; and yet we have a beautifully clear and distinct ability to think of and discourse about many "essences" quite abstract from the things in which we may have come to know them. We can not do this with either soul or matter. And still for the Aristotelian the ensouled body, the embodied soul, is the substance "in the truest sense." But physics, all science, is the endeavor both to dissect and to abstract what is really there in order to make it intelligible. Science as it grows wiser and more successful should bring us back again to all of the world from which it started, so as to make what is really there not only intelligible but understandable. It may sound odd to say that relativity and quantum physics are on the way to doing this; but I believe it is so. Are the still newer physics, such as parity and imparity and antimatter, on the same way? And the biophysics of ADN? And what else? I think so; but this is still in the making. At least much else has taken the élan of the Einstein-Bohr physics.

I was thinking the other day that we are fortunate to have so much narrative and description of the making of science in this century when I came across a paragraph deploring how little we have—that Einstein and Bohr and Pauli and Schrödinger and Szilard and many others are gone. There is truth in both feelings. But surely there have been an extraordinary number of books, especially in the last few years, mostly for the general reader—books like George Gamow's *Thirty Years that Shook Physics* and Barbara Lovett Cline's *Questioners: Physicists and the Quantum Theory* (recounted and reviewed at length in *The New Yorker* in 1966 by Jeremy Bernstein)—and many with pictures. To be sure we do not have the photographic record we have of movie, stage, and TV stars, of warriors or athletes or politicians; but we must not demand the impossible. And when we think what we have in the way of accounts of Copernicus, Vesalius, Galileo, Kepler, Bacon, Descartes, Harvey, Gilbert, Boyle, Newton, Huyghens, we may well be grateful.

Controversies frequently, if not regularly, get hotter, degenerate in quality, and are just put aside as people get tired of them or of the acrimony. In my boyhood before World War I there was a pleasant belief that understanding widens and deepens and tolerance grows. We are no longer apt to think so, but we can take some comfort that fashion and boredom can do for us something of what improved understanding was supposed to do. So of homoiousian against homoousian and supra- and infra-lapsarianism. Not a few lives were lost over each. The putting aside is a great worldly help, however theory may be postponed. Sometimes as theoretic controversy the rivalry is about the nature of a real or good thing, and the result is in a denial that the thing is. Is it true that X is a or that X is b? After a time let us, somewhat timidly, deny that there is any X. Then we go to other fields.

So I think it has happened twice, on large scale, with

"substance." Aristotle's debate, after a fine first sight in the *Categories* of the nature of prime substance, is so often and so convolutedly about whether substance is always prime substance, the thing; or may also be, or may contrarily be, matter or form; that philosophers, wearied and humble anyway after the three hundred years of the glory that was Greece, tried dogmatically to accept and then to put aside decision or to deny or ignore the actuality of substance.

After Descartes' unfortunate definition and his accent on extended substance for the sake of physics, argument rose and reached a pedestrian "height" in the Locke-Stillingfleet correspondence, which was radically deflected by the subordination of the question "What is substantial?" to the criterion of the helpfulness or otherwise to the contemporary Christian version of the immortality of the soul. It may be that out of this the imaginative originality of Berkeley brought his spiritualist substantialism. But Berkeley was slightly understood or misunderstood, and his immaterialism with respect to the objects of perception was promptly denatured by Hume into a denial of all substance.

Students sometimes ask what a Milesian "hylozoism"—an integral theory of the soul and body—does to a belief in immortality. They ask this especially after reading Aristotle, who uses just such a theory of soul to dismiss immortality (except now and then for the "purely rational," which does not give him sure evidence of a material organ and medium) and to deride the transmigration doctrine of Socrates, to whom in general he seems to me to be closer than Plato is. Well, this is another story. But I should be sorry to leave a barrier to any otherwise willing listener; and it may be enough to say that the difficulties are rather for our conventionally trained imaginations than insuperable in logic. Aristotle did not have his imagination trained to our conventions, but he had a very literal imagination (I would not change it) which sometimes made his own theories too literal, as it did sometimes in respect of this very theory of the soul as the "form of the body." He shuns any passage of the soul from one body to another as being like the passage of the insignia on a ring to the wax; but he denounces Democritus for supposing that the soul, that life, could possibly reside in any shape or arrangement or configuration of the material atoms in the void. The life of the body, he says better, is like the seeing of the eye: "the soul is the first entelechy of a body having life naturally within it." But sight is a function and does not seem to have the unity of even an eye when considered apart from the rest of its body; whereas the soul seems to be that which contributes individuality to the body, or if you prefer to say, as Aristotle would have preferred, the living individuality of the body is what we call soul. Can that in any meaningful way be thought to live after the end of this life, or to have lived before the birth of this life? It would seem to require—on the premise that life needs body and body needs life and that life and body are aspects of substance and not separate substances (this is leaving open the question whether there is lifeless matter; although such a doctrine might suggest, symmetrically, that there is an immaterial life)—a previous or subsequent life of the soul would seem to require either an instantaneous passage to another body, or a period of nonexistence between bodies, or more than one body or sorts of body of which the deaths are not simultaneous. The last might have been explored by Aristotle with his theory of the three souls and of reason without gross body. And it may be enough to add that there have been fairly many believers in body-soul mutuality —considering the much greater number of dualists, materialists, idealists—who have also been believers in immortality or continuance. Saint Paul was one; he seems to have been as sure he would have a body as he was uncontent with the one he had this time.

As a Christian I have suggested a Copenhagen interpretation of the dogma of the Trinity, a dogma that has delighted some, offended some (including Mr. Lovejoy), and puzzled many. Make up your mind whether light is a wave or a particle. Fresnel seemed to answer "crucially" in favor of wave. Now the quantum answers otherwise, without upsetting Fresnel. So Athanasian Christian experience finds three in one. The instrument we use to measure, the need and the path we go, do not give the nature found, but they seem to have something ineradicable to do with what person, hypostasis, continuity or discreteness, comes to answer. Perhaps such complementarity is our proper approach to any ultimate. (A further suggestion, from Athanasius—and from Kant—would be that Copenhagen physics might look for a third.)

A new edition of Mother Goose reminds me that she has a story for substance, which I use to end with:

> There was an old woman
> Lived under a hill;
> And if she's not gone
> She lives there still.

But then I think of more and more summings-up from the same source. Mother Goose is, indeed, a collection of very substantial poems.

INDEX

Designed by Edward King

Composed in Linotype Electra by The Colonial Press Inc.

Printed offset on P&S Old Forge by The Colonial Press Inc.

Bound in paper and cloth editions by The Colonial Press Inc.